# Kearns Boys

*Life Stories by
Six Brothers*

## <u>Dedication</u>

We would like to dedicate this book to the most wonderfully imperfect two people who to this day hold the highest levels of respect, admiration, and love in our hearts.

There are no words to describe the depth and breadth of our devotion and thankfulness we have for our parents:

**Thomas Walter Kearns**

**Elizabeth "Betty" Clare Kearns**

ISBN: 9798642567999
Copyright: Marysville, California 2020

## Table of Contents

## Forward

When our brother Pat suggested the six brothers collaborate and write a book based on random recollections of our experiences growing up, I wasn't sure what to expect. And certainly didn't anticipate learning anything new about my brothers. When it was suggested that we each write 10 stories, I thought that might be a stretch.

I wondered what the theme of the book would become. Stories that poked fun at each other? Stories that revealed a crazy sense of humor? Confessions of deeds better-kept secret? And could we even come up with ten stories each? I assumed some of the stories would include our parents but didn't expect the level of respect and love for them each brother went to great lengths to share. The book, and our lives, are a true testament for just how special they were. Is it rare that we six are all still friends and good friends at that? I may be biased but I think we are genuinely good people. Our morals are solid. Our respect for

God, family, and country are unshakable. These attributes can be traced directly to how we were raised by mom and dad.

Going into this project we each thought we knew our brothers. I know I didn't expect to learn anything new. After all, being the oldest, I was the only one who could claim that I was there for each of their entire lives…… As is often the case, how wrong I was. The ten-story goal did turn out to be a challenge, but only because it was hard to decide which ten stories to share. We have lived full lives for sure. And, admittedly, some stories are probably not appropriate for a "family" book – those will have to wait for volume two. We have led different lives and that is apparent in our writings, both style, and content. But I think there is a commonality in our sharings, it's clear we each have a love for family and each other.

One unexpected outcome from this effort is a newfound desire to learn more about my brothers. I know there is so much I missed, and these stories reveal glimpses of some pretty entertaining guys. Unlike our friends, we don't choose our brothers. In our case though, I can't imagine not having any of the five as my brothers. And I would also choose each one of them as my friends. Sure, we still argue, and at times a disagreement might create some distance, but it never lasts and that is the beauty of being family.

I hope as you read through this compilation of happy, sad, embarrassing, thankful, blessed times of our lives, you will also get a glimpse of just what a great job Tom and Betty, our parents, did to set us on the right course. God truly blessed us.

Kevin

## <u>Chapter 1</u>

## Prunes, Race Trucks, And Mythical Rabbits- Kevin

Growing up in an agricultural area, it was quite common for "summer work" to somehow involve fruit. Especially when we were younger and not being old enough to possess a driver's license made the thought of venturing out to secure a job on our own a dream that would have to wait a few years.

When I was fourteen years old, the age range of the six boys ran from me to the youngest brother Dan, who was two at that time. Our Dad usually taught summer school, which was a blessing for him since he could stay indoors during the many days that reached the high ninety degrees and often, north of 100. This only lasted part of the summer though and once the summer session ended, Mom was more than ready to get a break from staying home watching all 6 boys. Since Dad taught practically year-round this was her only chance to get out, even still, she took the opportunity to help a few of us experience the value of a strong work ethic.

Picking prunes was about the only work that unskilled boys could hope for at those young ages, but even that menial work had a minimum age. I was 14, Tim was 12 and Terry was 10, which was the cut-off. Pat, Mike, and Dan were still too young, so they missed all the fun and stayed home with Dad. Mom had to convince the orchard boss to let us pick as a family. I think he knew we would be lucky to fill even one bin a day, but since we were sent out to gather the fruit that was left behind after the shaker had collected the majority, what did he have to lose. I think he also felt a little sorry for us but respected our desire to try. Mom was required to drive us out there each day and stay with us as our "supervisor" so we were just an afterthought anyway.

We were not very good at picking the prunes off the ground. It was slow work and we were either in a bent-over position or down on our knees with our buckets. The hardened clods of dirt pressed through our thinned jeans and it was hard to decide which was worse, our sore backs or painful knees. I guess it didn't matter, we soon had both anyway. Now, mom was not good at picking, not at all. God bless her for spending those days in the hot orchards with us just so we could earn a little money. We were equally fortunate they didn't charge us for the fruit she ate. She easily consumed more than she picked and by midday, she often could be found sitting against a tree, in the shade, catching a bit of shut-eye. Well, not just sitting since you probably know what effect prunes can have on the digestive tract, but that's a story for another time.

Now, normally we would just continue to work through Mom's nap. But one day I decided to try my hand at driving the truck. I didn't have a license, but dad had let me steer a few times and come on….if Mom could do it, so could I. Gently disturbing mom from her dreamscape, I mentioned I needed to go get water and whether she realized that meant I was taking the truck, I didn't wait to clarify. Tim and Terry were both eager to take a break from picking and jumped at the chance to share in the adventure. I slid in behind the wheel, Tim into the passenger side, and Terry hopped into the bed of the little Datsun pickup. The orchard was pretty isolated so no one would be able to see us, and the bordering gravel road stretched for quite a long way. I'm sure we weren't going nearly as fast as it felt, but the thrill added to the perception of many additional miles per hour. After driving for several minutes, we decided to turn around and head back. For some unknown reason at the time, we yelled at Terry to change from standing in the bed of the truck, and join us in the cab. Although seat belts were never a consideration, our three bodies jammed together would prove lifesaving in very short order. Confidence in my superior driving skills overflowing now, I decided to pick up the pace. Little did I know that gravel, sharp right turns and excessive speed would result in such a rude awakening. Halfway into the turn, which was halfway too late, the centrifugal force caused our truck to assume anything but an upright position. When we came to a stop, we got out, and still in shock, we were just thankful that Terry had made the move to the front. He surely would have been killed when we flipped over, or hurt very badly at best, so looking back I'm sure divine intervention held us securely in the palm of His hand.

With nothing more than bruises, my ego getting the worst of it, we now had to face Mom. And scarier, eventually Dad. How are we going to explain an innocent water gathering effort resulting in totaling our only family transportation? I had the brilliant idea to blame it on the rabbit that ran in front, causing me to swerve out of the way to protect his life. Mom loved animals, she would surely understand. We walked back to her sleeping tree and shared our story. I don't know if she believed us, but her love for her sons focused on being thankful we were ok. I don't remember how mom was able to reach Dad, this was long before cell phones. And I have no idea how we got home since there wasn't a second family car. But I do recall thinking we were out of the woods since my story of the rascally Wabbit being the culprit seemed unquestioned. That is until we had to make the police report for the insurance claim. We had to go into the police station to make the report and I quickly found myself eye to eye, nose to nose with the policeman, who just wasn't seeming to want to accept my story. He kept asking me the same questions repeatedly, and then pulled out a thick, black book filled with "laws". He asked me to read one paragraph that simply said something along the lines of it being unlawful to lie to a policeman. He then asked me again about the rabbit and I tearfully confessed there was no rabbit. It had been a squirrel. No, just kidding, I expressed sorrow for lying and took full responsibility. I think they knew all along, but they played it well.

I expected Dad to throw the book at me. At the very least, swing the family wooden paddle a few times. But Dad being Dad, the amazing, loving father God blessed us with, he simply expressed his disappointment that I lied, and said I would have to find a way to repay the insurance deductible. And then he hugged me and said how thankful he was that I wasn't hurt, that none of his boys were hurt.

I don't think I ever paid that deductible. And I never look at prunes the same way. I am a little more cautious on gravel roads to this day. But most of all, I am just thankful Terry got in the front seat.

### Chapter 2

## On My Own – Tim

My brothers and I grew up in a small town and it seemed like all the families of the kids we grew up with knew each other.  It was very comfortable growing up with the same people from elementary school through high school.  Gaining more and more friends as the school population grew at each level.

Growing up this way, made us feel safe and built lots of confidence. My brothers and I were popular and excelled in school and sports.  We were "big fish" in a small pond.

After high school and bouncing in between junior college and working in the peach/pear orchards as tractor divers, my younger brother Terry and I decided to go into the military. It seemed like we were stagnating in our progression into independent adulthood in our hometown.  Terry and I went to the recruiting office and marched into the Air Force branch.  A couple of our neighbors (directly across the street and another two houses down on the corner) were in the Air Force and stationed at Beale Air Force base only a few miles down the road. We were both excited to join, but then were asked by the recruiter if we had ever been in any trouble.  He said that the retention rate in the Air Force at that time was at an all-time high and that they were only accepting recruits that had a spotless record. Well, that knocked me out as I had been in a little trouble in junior high and high school.  Terry might have also, although probably not. Regardless, we wanted to join the same branch of service. I believe he told us to check with the Navy recruiter at the next office over because that is where we ended up and they were more than happy to sign us up. We went to the Oakland MEPS (Military Entrance Processing Station) to take a written test and a physical. We both passed and signed up for the DEP "Delayed Entry Program."  This gave us about six months before we had to go to boot camp. Terry signed up for the "storekeeper" rating and his school would be in Meridian, MS. I wanted to be an underwater welder or demolition person, but I am colorblind, so I couldn't do those jobs. They told me just to go into bootcamp and choose a job while there.

My brother and I were lucky enough to sign up for the "buddy" program. This let us go to the same bootcamp together.  Since my brother's "A" school for storekeeper was in Meridian, MS, he was going to be sent to Orlando, Florida for bootcamp. Well, we were on the buddy program, so I went there also. It was great having Terry with me in bootcamp because with both of us there together, we were not lonely. We were going through the same experiences together.  I finally figure out a job I could do being colorblind. I was going to be a Personnelman.  I would learn computers and work pretty much on "paperwork." Well, wouldn't you know it, the Personnelman "A" school just happened to be in Meridian, MS also, so after

Bootcamp, Terry and I went for the next few weeks, together again, to the Navy base in Meridian. This was much better just going to school each day and then goofing off together at the end of each day.  This was much different than boot camp.

After "A" school, I received orders to San Diego, CA to serve aboard the Aircraft carrier, USS Kitty Hawk. Well, wouldn't you know it, Terry received orders to the Kitty Hawk also, and this was for the next three years for us. We were so happy. Then the hammer fell. Terry was signed up for the TAR program (training active reserves). He would not be able to serve on the Kitty Hawk, but his orders were switched to Naval Reserve Center in Colorado Springs, CO. Oh no, we would be on our own. Well after a short leave (vacation) at home, I headed out to San Diego with my older brother Kevin. We drove to San Diego, over the Coronado Bridge, and into the naval station where the ships are located. We parked and walked up to this enormous warehouse that towered above us and stretched out to the left and the right for hundreds of yards.  We asked each other "where is the ship?" We had to walk back to get the entire picture.  That enormous warehouse WAS the ship.  It was that big! I felt my stomach drop to the floor.  This is where I will live for the next 3 years? When I finally said "goodbye" to my brother was when I finally left all familiarity behind. This feeling of aloneness was almost overwhelming. I must have prayed to God for strength because what happened after I walked up the "ladder" to one of the ship's plane elevators and was introduced to someone to get me to my quarters, where the nearest "head" was, where the galley was, etc., I was on an adventure that lasted for 8 years.

Voluntarily or forced, to venture out and "grow up" is a bit painful, but not doing it would have been a shame. The adventures in different counties, from skydiving to scuba diving, and all the amazing experiences wouldn't seem to be possible without breaking away from that "safety" of home and just going for it.

## <u>Chapter 3</u>

### Driveway Basketball - Terry

Growing up on Jeffery Court was a dream come true for someone that loved playing hoops. Our driveway 3-on-3 games would go on all day. The games would be the first team to score 10 baskets would win then everyone else would line up to shoot from the free-throw line to see who would play the winners. The first three people to make a basket were the next team-up. If you had a good three-person team you could stay out there playing all day. The only refreshment was water from the garden hose as we never had any money in those days.

I remember that we all thought we had the best skills around, and we seemed to never get tired. Those games would draw big crowds on many occasions, and they would be quite competitive. The highlight of our day would be when our father would come home from work and motion for the ball. Someone would pass him the ball at the back of the driveway and my father would do his famous backslide shot and sink it to all our delight. We would all cheer at his smooth touch and then continue playing. Those times are always going to be some of my fondest moments.

## Chapter 4

### The Fragility Of Life – Pat

It seems as if it were just yesterday, at least by the measure of the clarity of the picture that I hold in my mind. I was sixteen years of age and worked on a large fruit ranch during the summer. I drove what they called a Bin Carrier and earned $5.25 an hour. The unusual-looking machine had a driver's seat mounted on the left side of the vehicle and possessed large balloon-like tires. There were two chain-driven tracks that ran from front to back of the vehicle that could hold six full-size fruit bins. The vehicle was also equipped with a hydraulic mechanism that raised and lowered the front forks and drove the chains. One was able to speed through the peach and pear orchards and strategically drop off and stagger empty bins for the picking crews and then return later once the bins were filled with fruit and scoop them up and deliver them to the packing sheds. It was usual for each Bin Carrier driver to support 5-7 picking crews. The work was dusty, fast-paced, and exciting. It was the perfect job for an adolescent with little critical thinking skills, and just enough constant stimulation to make the work hours fly by.

Picking season meant that there was work that needed to be done seven days a week, and the days lasted from sunup to almost sundown. Working the ranch during the summers consumed our lives.

Dantoni Ranch was where the whole family worked, at least during the summers. It was almost a rite of passage for a Kearns to devote at least a few summers to the work and way of life. It was one way we all learned about responsibility, reliability, and work ethic. Although, we were Kearns and we did often find ways to cut corners, slack here and there, and mess things up from time to time. Not only did most of my brothers work at the ranch, but our friends did as well.

This particular day started just like many of the rest. I awoke early in the morning before the sun had begun to shine. I dressed and brushed my teeth. I made two ham and cheese sandwiches for lunch and grabbed a Carnation Breakfast Bar to eat on the way. The mornings were cool, so I dressed in a warm jacket and donned winter gloves. After placing my helmet over my head, I sat upon and started the engine of my Yamaha 500 motorcycle that I had recently brought from my brother, Terry. The exhaust pipes must have rusted, or at least the baffles because if I reeved the engine too much, flames would blast out from the pipes. I didn't mind, I thought it was rather cool.

The long road that led to the ranch was named Danotni Road, and it must have been at least 4 miles long. Halfway down the road it veered slightly to the left and rose and fell over a hill with a small turnoff road at the top of the hill. The twisting of the road and the small hill obscured the view of oncoming traffic. I had never seen anyone use the turnoff road at the top of the hill, and we usually used the small hill as an opportunity to speed and see if we could catch some air on our motorcycles. It was a daily quest of mine to see just how many micro-seconds I could get the wheels off the ground.

As I drove to work, I didn't see anyone else ahead of me or behind me. I began to wonder if I was late for work, or just early. Suddenly, as I approached the hill, I noticed one of my friends with his truck parked on top of the hill and pointing in the direction of the turnoff road. He was pacing back and forth and seemed to be in distress. I cautiously road my bike up to him and as soon as I removed my helmet, I could hear him saying, "I just didn't see him. I didn't see him?" I had no idea what he was talking about until I saw him. On the opposite side of the hill, there was a motorcycle twisted and crashed with pieces scattered along the road. Lying in the middle of the road was a body. I recognized the motorcycle and body immediately. It was Steve, one of my brother's good friends and a fellow worker at the ranch. I rushed towards him. As I advanced, I came across a large object in mostly one piece. It was his brain. I only glanced, but the shape and characteristics were indisputable. It was a brain. It looked exactly like the pictures of a brain I had seen before with bumps and crevices. I raced toward the body and although I could see Steve's face, the top of his head was gone. There were no mandatory helmet laws in California at the time. Even with my untrained eye, I knew he was dead. He had no brain. I removed my jacket and covered Steve's head. I then ran back to my friend who was still pacing and asked, "What happened?" He shouted, "I didn't see him until it was too late. I turned at the top of the hill and just then I saw him. He was trying to lay the bike down, but he went right under my truck. It ripped his brain right out." He then began to cry and fell to his knees. I had no words of comfort or wisdom. I just couldn't believe this had happened. I had never known anyone to die. It felt like an eternity of quiet and darkness but was probably only a matter of minutes when others arrived at the site of the accident, people older than me. Someone must have driven and called the police because they, too, showed up a few minutes later with lights and sirens.

The rest of the day was and still is a blur. I don't remember additional details, but I do remember with as much clarity today as the day it occurred the fully formed and complete brain sitting in the middle of the road, and our friend laying there without the top of his head. It was then that I realized that life is more fragile than I thought, and that in an instant our time here on earth could be done. An accident can happen at any time and even if one did nothing wrong life could cease without warning.

Lesson learned is that life is fragile, and to live as if it might be our last day. Also, be ready if God wants to call us home sooner than planned.

## Chapter 5

## My Superhero Dad - Mike

Growing up in a family of boys (I'm number 5 out of 6) is very competitive, especially when all five of your brothers are better at sports than you! I tried hard but never had the natural ability that the other brothers had.

My Dad was our biggest supporter. He would never miss a baseball game, a football or basketball game. One must understand the significance of this. He taught five days a week as a middle school teacher during the day and worked a second job teaching numerous nights each week as an adult education teacher. He was a Machine!

Since I could never make the starting teams in school, I had to do what I could to try and make my Dad proud. I went out for the swimming team and was even the president of the Swim Team/Club one year. All my life I have thought about this and it still bothers me to some degree today. Did I embarrass my Dad? First of all, I was overweight in High School and we had to wear the required "Speedo" bathing suit. My "Fat Roll" would lap over my "Panties" and extra skin would hang. Visualize it...Pretty Sexy! Then when we had to get up on the platform and lean over right before you dive in, I'm sure my Dad was proud of me at that point. NOT!! I never won a race, but I finished every race which allowed us to get points. I even did the 20-lap race! It was so tiring! If my Dad was embarrassed he never let me know. It never showed. He continued to come to my races, so I guess he wasn't too embarrassed. That's my Dad...My Superhero!!

I think some of my proudest moments were at the dinner table growing up. I remember just cracking my Dad up so bad that he would start coughing and laughing while crying at the same time. I would do these impressions of characters I made up, mixed in with jokes. To see my Dad get such enjoyment out of my comedy meant the world to me. That thought still brings me such comfort and joy. Even though he has been gone for years now, I still "Talk" to him every day.

## Chapter 6

### Peanut Butter And Jelly - Dan

Growing up at the time that we did, kids were able to be kids. What I mean by that is, we played outside with our friends from sunrise to sunset. Riding bikes, playing tag, shooting hoops, and whiffle ball games in the street in front of my house. So many amazing memories.

After the hours of nonstop playing, it was a guarantee that my Mom would come through with her award-winning peanut butter and jelly sandwiches. We became dependent on it. There was no better way to wash it down than lining up for a big chug from the garden hose.

Our mom's greatest pleasure in life was taking care of people. She loved her boys and was always there for us to talk to. Especially when we feared that we would be in trouble with our dad for something we did. I would go to her to help soften the blow ahead of time knowing that maybe she would go to our dad ahead of time and take the pressure off.

Mom was so interested in everybody's lives. Whether we had a girlfriend or any friend over, she would ask so many questions about them. I would shake my head as if to say, here we go again. It got to the point that I would warn them ahead of time. Eventually, I just referred to my mom as "20 questions".

My mother cared so much for kids that she had an entire hall closet full of toys. This would be for any of the neighborhood kids to come over and play. This would continue even after all of us were raised. She eventually consolidated it to a single bottom drawer in the kitchen and would allow each kid to take one home. I don't think any toy had a value over a dollar.

My friends and I liked to compare my family, especially my parents, to the Cleavers. My mom specifically as June Cleaver. She lived her life, loving her kids and the friends that came with us. She reserved her biggest love and dedication to our father, however. Every morning without fail, she would wake up and cook my dad a full breakfast which included scrambled eggs, bacon, and toast. Then she would pack his lunch for him to brown bag it to work. What an amazing soul she was.

## <u>Chapter 7</u>

### Pillowcase Backpack - Kevin

We didn't grow up poor. We were rich in so many ways. We had two very loving parents who married as young sweethearts and stayed married their entire lives. When dad passed away, at some point we asked Mom if she would ever remarry and she said of course not. Dad and Jesus were the only Men she needed in her life. And the riches were exemplified in many other ways. We had decent schools, my brothers and I were blessed with above-average athleticism. Some of the brothers were way above average, even bordering on great (not me).

God played a very healthy role in our lives. All in all, we were wealthy in many ways, just not money or materialistic possessions. Don't get me wrong, our house was decent, we had daily meals consistently, and we did seem to always have a functional car. But there was only so much our Dad could provide working as a teacher and supporting a full-time homemaking wife and six boys.

The thing is, we lived in an area where our financial standing didn't matter to most people. And I think, as a result, we didn't notice that we probably had less than most of the others when it came to possessions. We stayed pretty close to home, close to each other, so it just never was apparent. Well, most of the time that is.

Time does a great job sanding the rough edges of growing up. Most memories meld together, and recollection is usually balanced overall with remembering growing up as typically pretty good. There are some occasions though that forever stand out. I remember preparing for my first scout camping trip. I had never camped in my life, and the thought of venturing out and spending a night away from home seemed awesome. We were told to "pack" certain essentials and meet on Saturday in the school parking lot to load up. I had zero experience preparing, so I asked my dad what I should do. I told him I thought I needed a backpack, but he suggested that might be too much since it was just one night. He tossed me a pillowcase and said I could easily fit anything I needed to bring inside, and it would be lighter and easier to carry. Looking back, I know he just didn't have any extra money to buy a backpack, but at the time I had no clue, so I just believed him.

Saturday morning arrived and I grabbed my pillowcase backpack and raced to the school parking lot. Everyone was working together to load all the gear into the back of the pickup trucks. When it came time for me to hand my "pack" to the guy loading, I was happy to see it was one of my very good friends,

Jay. He took it from me and slung it over to another guy who would catch it and stack it with the others. Everything was going great until that second guy caught my "pack" and shouted out, what the heck is this, a pillowcase?! I don't know why I hadn't noticed until then, everyone else had backpacks except me. My friend Jay quickly yelled at the guy that it was my backpack, shut up, and just load it with the rest. I will always remember that moment fondly and thankful he was there. As life would have it, the rest of the trip went well and there weren't any consequences with my pillowcase.

Oddly, the impact of that experience would be felt, not that weekend, but much later, and many times in fact. Although the pillowcase had almost no impact that weekend, many times later in life I reflect on that time. Reflecting on how my Dad must have felt like he let me down a little by not being able to afford a real backpack. I wish I could have told him then not to worry and that he already provided more than anyone could hope for, more than I could ever thank him for. And the older I got, the more I came to appreciate what he did for us and how "wealthy" we were. I also find myself remembering that even though I must have stood out as the pillowcase backpacker, that occasion came and went, had no ill effect on my life, and life just carried on. At times when I start to worry that I might stand out for the wrong reasons, or might not be measuring up to someone else's standards, I think it's probably just my imagination. And even if it's not, who cares, in time no one will remember anyway. Besides, that was a very cool pillowcase.

## Chapter 8

### Isolation

I was working in Silicon Valley in the computer industry during its boom just after the turn of the millennium. After working a few years in San Jose, the "dot.com" industry, for the most part, crashed and many people lost their jobs. I was one of them. My youngest brother Dan was doing well financially up in Redding, California in real estate finance. He suggested that I join him up there and work for the broker with which he was employed. My oldest brother had a big house about 30 miles northeast of Redding in the small town of Montgomery Creek. This house remained vacant except for a few visits a year on vacation. This house was a mile back off a small-town road and was in the middle of a forest. This property was 30 acres with a beautiful 2500 sq. ft house on it. Living pretty much off the grid and in the middle of the forest was like a dream come true to me, but my wife, Angela, felt the opposite. We had one small powerline that ran from the road back to the house. There was no gas, propane, or cable TV. There was no city water or sewer. At the highest elevation of the property was a well. We had an electric pump that would pump the water up from the well and into a small water tank. Then the water flowed down the water lines to the house only powered by gravity. Surprising, the water pressure was pretty strong. We had a septic tank for our sewer receptacle out behind the house and a company would have to come out and remove the waste from the septic tank periodically. We had an old-time wood-burning stove downstairs and a fireplace upstairs. We used these two every day in the winter as electricity was so expensive and we had 30 acres of forest to gather all the wood we needed. My wife Angela, two of our boys (Richard and Robbie) and I lived here in the house. We kept the boys busy on the coldest nights feeding the wood-burning stove throughout the night.

Our first winter opened our eyes to the excitement and pitfalls of living so far away from the rest of the town. The snow looked so beautiful and romantic falling on the cars and the porch. Everything was turning white. We had been to the snow many times, but we had never lived where it snowed. Finally, we went to bed and when we woke the next day everything was covered in snow. At first glance, it looks mesmerizing. We thought "this is fantastic, what a view." Until we tried to leave for work that day. The heavens dumped almost three feet of snow overnight. Although I had a four-wheel-drive truck (I didn't have chains at the time), we were not able to traverse down the path leading out to the road. The house sat down a little hill at the end of the path, so trying to climb out of this hill was no use. We just kept sliding back. We didn't know what to do. We had a phone and could call Dan (as he lived in Redding), but his car wouldn't be able to travel down this one-mile path either. Well, little did we know that a few acres away from our property, a farmer had his land and it butted up against ours. He had a feeling, with us being new up there, that we might be in trouble with this storm. He showed up at our fence line with his old-time tractor, with huge wheels and a scoop bucket on the front. Angela, the kids, and I were able to jump in the bucket and he carried us all the way out to the road. Dan was able to come and retrieve us and we stayed with him until the snow melted enough for us to get back to the house. This taught us a lesson. Subsequently, whenever we would start to get heavy snow, it was Richard and Robbie's task to drive the truck up and down the mile path to keep shaving down the built-up snow on the road throughout the night.

Here is another exciting event we had while out on the property. We had a couple of Labrador retrievers (Shasta and Lassen – named for the largest mountains in Northern California). We would leave their dogfood out 24/7 and they would just eat when they were hungry. They ran around the property constantly and stayed in very good shape. Angela and I had our bedroom upstairs and Richard and Robbie had theirs downstairs. Well, one morning, we heard the dogs going crazy. Nonstop barking downstairs in the backyard (which remember was forest). Richard ran upstairs and yelled, "there's a bear at my window!" We couldn't believe it but ran downstairs to see, sure enough, a huge black bear was standing on his hind legs and trying to tear apart an old swamp cooler that was in the boys' bedroom window. What seemed to have happened is that squires or rats had taken some of the dog food and hid it inside the old swamp cooler. The bear could smell this and wanted it. With us yelling at him and the dogs' constant barking, we were able to get the bear to retreat out into the forest about 40 yards. He then just faced us and sat there. Luckily

Kevin had left one of his 9mm handguns at the house and I was able to go out on the porch and shoot right beside his head. I took a few shots and although he didn't want to move at first, he finally retreated. Well, we got that old swamp cooler, threw it in the back of the truck, and took it to the other side of the property. We didn't see this bear again, but while hiking the property a couple of weeks later, we saw the swamp cooler had been torn apart and rolled down the hill. The bear must have found it.

I hope to one day live in the country again … I wonder what adventures await us this next time.

## <u>Chapter 9</u>

## Summer Vacation - Terry

Every summer my when my five brothers and I were quite young we would get to go to Santa Cruz for vacation. This trip would be a day trip or if we were lucky, we would spend one night at the Holiday Inn.

This trip would begin with five of us boys in the back of my dad's Datsun "little hustler" pickup with a camper shell. One lucky brother would sit upfront with my mom and dad. When we arrived, we would go to the beach boardwalk and we could ride all the exciting rides. We felt like we were on top of the world.

In the afternoon we would go to the beach and try body surfing and play in the ocean for hours. In the evening we would either head back home or go to the motel. If we were lucky enough to stay the evening, we would then swim in the motel pool, and the next day we would go back home.

Even though these trips were very short they were one of the highlights of my summer. I know with eight people in our household and money very tight at times, I will always have a deep appreciation for my parents making the trip each year. We never complained about the duration of these trips, we just loved going as a family.

## Chapter 10

### Loneliness – Pat

Growing up in a tiny three-bedroom and one-bathroom house with six brothers and parents left little room or opportunity to feel alone or lonely. There was always something occurring and people and activity around. And if that wasn't enough stimulation, you could always walk outside to the world and energy of Jeffery Court. We lived on a small residential court with probably twenty homes, and most of them had children eager to play at almost any hour. Our house seemed to be magnetic in drawing others to our driveway. It was in that driveway and front yard that plans were constantly being made for the neighborhood, playing basketball, touch football in the street, Frisbee tag, hide and go seek, etc.

It wasn't until I finished high school and joined the Navy that I had my first extended experience of being away from all that was familiar in my life. For the first time, I was in a place and situation without a completion date six sight, and where I knew no one and no one knew me.

Bootcamp was interesting, being thrown together with people of all races and ethnic groups, as well as from all different parts of the country. I even remember there being quite a few young black men from the east coast who never learned how to swim. That just blew my mind. How could anyone not know how to swim? What did they do all summer?

I did eventually make a few friends in Bootcamp, but those friendships did not have the depth of childhood friendships. There was no shared history, and we all knew the connection was temporary. I did discover the value of letter writing and being able to express interior feelings and emotions and better yet, that receiving a letter was a reward beyond belief. It was a connection with someone and something familiar. The highlight of the day was in the late afternoon when classes were over, exercise and drills had been accomplished, and everyone was sitting on the concrete slab spit shining their boots, and mail call was being announced. All ninety of us were waiting with anticipating hope that our name would be called and that a letter had arrived.

After Bootcamp, I was assigned to attend Hospital Corpsman School in San Diego near Balboa Park. I had packed my seabag with everything I owned and took a bus to the base. By the time I arrived, it was dark outside. I recall being in uniform, my dress blues, and wearing the oversized seabag on my back. I walked up to the entrance gate and showed my military ID to the guards. They allowed me to enter and directed me to follow the road to the rear of the base to the barracks. The walk must have been almost two miles. No one else could be seen on the road and there must not have been much of a moon since it appeared significantly darker than previous evenings. It was during that walk that a powerful feeling of loneliness overcame me. I questioned, what have I done? Is this really what I thought joining the Navy as my brothers had done would be like? The remainder of the walk was painful as my mind swirled with negativity. I eventually arrived at the barracks and asked for the quartermaster. The young man greeted me and assigned me a room. That was it. I now had a room, but I was on my own to figure the rest out.

That night of loneliness was the start of a journey. Breaking away from childhood and entering adulthood. The comfort of familiarity had been lost and a new adventure awaited. It didn't take long for me to learn that life could be what I made of it. I had the choice to sit back and wait for something to happen, or I could go seeking it. As an introvert, I would tend to sit back, contemplate, and wait, but intellectually I knew that would not be a solution to loneliness.

One needs a sense of familiarity in their lives, and they also need friends. Comfort comes from knowing what to expect and having people in your life that you can expect things from. This expectation doesn't need to be self-serving, although it might be on some level. Being a friend also means caring for another, loving them, and being there for them even if you do not care to be there at the time. It is devotion. It is love. It is being present.

Lesson learned – Loneliness at times cannot be avoided, maybe even necessary to learn and to appreciate, but it can be counteracted.

## Chapter 11

## "DIEGO" - Mike

I graduated High School in June of 1987. Two months later I was in the Navy in Boot Camp in San Diego.  I was going to be a Religious Program Specialist (RP) like my brother Tim. After Boot camp I went to my "A" school in San Francisco to learn how to run the Church office. On the last day of school, they were giving out our next assignments and when they got to me, they said, "You're going to Diego!" I thought great. I get to stay in California! I said, "I Love San Diego!" The instructor laughed and said, "Not San Diego, you're going to Diego Garcia!" I asked where in the world that was and he grabbed a Globe and spun it around. He pointed to a dot in the middle of the Indian Ocean 10,800 miles away from Marysville. I was going to be FAR AWAY!

Diego Garcia is a tropical island in the middle of the Persian Gulf. No dependents are allowed and tours were one year long. Phone calls were $4.00 a minute! After my one year was up I received orders back to Southern California as I was stationed with the Marine Corps at Camp Pendleton in Oceanside California. I had to go through their School of Infantry and wear the Marine Cammie's. My brother Tim was also with the Marines in Okinawa Japan. He later joined me at Camp Pendleton. We also met up in Saudi Arabia (see Tim's story) during Operation Desert Storm. I was scared it was the last time I would see him! We all thought we were going to get "Gassed." Thank God we did not.

## <u>Chapter 12</u>

**Sports And A Dad's Love – Dan**

I remember growing up in my family meant that you were active, kept busy, and played sports. I loved playing sports. As a young kid, maybe five or six years old, I remember being part of a track club called Peach Bowl Pacers. We would race against other clubs. That was fun, but the joy for me began when I started team sports. My first introduction to that life was when I was eight years old, playing little league baseball. I was hooked. I would continue through high school, focused on football, baseball, and basketball. The thought of competition was such a rush. However, an even bigger high was making my Dad proud.

Dad was an athlete himself, and he loved watching his boys play. He may have missed a game here and there between teaching all day and then sometimes teaching night school, but not many many. I vividly remember that our baseball games in high school would start right after 4 pm. I was always the leadoff batter. Without fail, as the opponent's pitcher was warming up and I was timing my swings, my Dad would be behind the backstop offering me words of encouragement. No different were my basketball and football games. I would look in the stands, hoping he was there. Of course, he was.

For as much as our Dad enjoyed watching his boys play, he never would attend the end of the season awards banquets. I would ask him why. He said that it made him too nervous wondering if we would win or not. He preferred to wait up at home in his living room chair, waiting for us to enter the front door.

I would be so excited when I would win an MVP trophy, partly because it was a great accomplishment to be recognized, but more so because I could see how proud I made my Dad.

## <u>Chapter 13</u>

## Dreams Are Fun, But Reality Usually Wins – Kevin

I learned of a horse auction that was coming up and got excited about the possibility of acquiring a great horse. The situation was not ideal due to the shelter at home restrictions related to Covid-19, so this auction would be held completely online. The ranch was a very well known, respectable source for good horses, but good sense recommends seeing the horse before you buy. Especially because there are no returns. And this ranch is in Wyoming, so getting there would be a bit tricky. Nonetheless, they seemed to have nice horses, one in particular, so I thought I would try.

I figured since the auction was only online, and virtual buying probably was considered risky by most, that maybe this was a chance to get a bargain. I don't have much experience buying horses, but I thought if I set my budget "reasonable" for the risk, what could I lose. I decided $8K would be my max bid, a bit of a stretch financially but if I could get "Monte", my favored horse, it would be worth the risk.

The day came for the auction. I had been up all night, imagining I would surely get "Monte" since I was willing to go all the way up to $8K. I wrestled with trying to find answers to all the questions…how would I get him home to California from Wyoming, where would I put him, how would I explain to my trainer that I bought him online when she had consistently told me that was insane…… My brother Tim and Partner Carol gathered with me around the computer, ready to start the bidding. We had drinks and snacks and were preparing to celebrate. We were all nervous….and then the bidding began. Well, I'm not sure if I ever saw the $8K mark come and go, but in no time, Monte had sold for over $40K!! Apparently, that is not uncommon for these horses, but I had no idea. I vacillated between disappointment and embarrassment. Dreaming had been fun, but reality kicked me in the shins for sure.

Oddly though, that experience awoke a memory that I had buried deep and had long forgotten. It took me back over 50 years, back to my cub scout days. Pinewood derby days specifically. That time is a bit bleary, somewhat fuzzy, but certain events remain crystal clear. Pinewood Derby is one of those.

Social media at the time consisted mainly of the telephone and the US mail, so until the day of the derby race, no one would know what anyone else was doing and each person's racecar was a secret only to be unveiled when time to compete. I can remember working so hard on that car. Night after night carving from a single block of wood, sanding every angle, doing anything I could to make it lighter and more aerodynamic. My dad wanted to help, but I was confident I had the knack. And parents helping wasn't supposed to be allowed anyway. I remember painting it red, a bright, fiery red.  Looking back, I had no idea what I was doing, and at most, followed the directions to build the most basic of cars. But what did I know? I had no one to compare to, no baseline with which to measure. My brothers were all younger, so no one had ventured down this road yet. What I did have though, was a very active imagination. I just knew I would win. I was going to crush the competition. Everyone would want me to help them build their cars next year. My dad was going to be so proud of me. I was definitely going to be the talk of the competition.

Race day came and I recall wrapping up my car, taking great care not to scratch the paint or throw off the alignment of the plastic wheels. The race was at Johnson Park School, our neighborhood school only a few blocks away. So, I walked there, anxious with excitement, barely containing myself. I would try to be somewhat humble when I won. Wanting to be sensitive to how hard others probably worked on their cars. But no promises….

As I entered the school gym, I was dumbfounded. Where did all these beautiful cars come from? Why did mine all of a sudden look so plain? Surely their fathers must have helped. Heck, they must have used all their aerospace engineering talent to take over and build their darn cars. Well, maybe mine didn't stand out in the looks department, but we did still have to race them. Confidence a bit battered, I was still hopeful mine would be competitive in the speed department. Maybe even place for an award. We set our cars on the top of the track, fingers crossed, and praying silently that God would give mine a bit of a push. Not a lot, just enough to win. I would stay humble, I promised Him. Ready, set go, and off they went. Wow, they went fast. Not mine, all the others.

Amazing how quickly reality stole the show. I'm glad all my hopes, my optimistic wishful thinking ahead of time had been my secret. My embarrassment would be something only I would know, but it hurt. I remember gathering my car and walking home. I did not walk fast but I remember thinking I was still traveling faster than my speed racer had made it down that track.

Walking through the front door, I was met by my Dad. He just smiled and commended me for doing my best. I don't know why for sure, but for some reason, at that moment, everything was ok.

I think it is still important to dream. Pursuing lofty goals, setting your bar high, and reaching is a good thing. Funny how two incidents, several decades apart, would still underscore that ultimately reality still wins out in the end. But we can have fun along the way. And maybe there is a lesson or two to be learned besides not having me build your pinewood derby car.

# <u>Chapter 14</u>

## Brothers Find Each Other In A Far-Off Land – Tim

Many of my brothers and I served in the military and we have many stories to tell of those adventures.  From living on ships, out at sea for months at a time, boot camps, infantry training, dangling on lines from helicopters, living in jungles, deserts, etc., let's leave those stories for another time. The tale I want to tell today is of a unique and awesome experience that both my brother Mike and I shared.

We were sent to Saudi Arabia to fight in the Gulf War.  He was in a tank battalion and I served in I MEF (1st Marine Expeditionary Force – [1st SRIG – surveillance reconnaissance intelligence group]). My job was the be the Navy Chaplain's bodyguard and right-hand man. This was Mike's job also in his unit serving hundreds of miles away. The US forces had a small group of communication personnel hunkered down with all the different allied troops that were on "our side" helping take down Saddam Hussein and the Iraqi forces. Our guys would be able to radio our fighter pilots to come to where we were located and fire on the enemy. This didn't always work as one time we were up in the most northern town in Saudi on the Kuwait border (Khafaji) when we saw the Iraqi troops coming at us in the distance and we called our air support to mow them down. Well, they didn't come as they were busy fighting elsewhere, so we had to hightail it out of there and when we returned later, the town was riddled with bullet holes. The Chaplain and I would hop into our Humvee with an encrypted radio and a GPS and head out into the desert. The Chaplain would drive, and I would be the passenger with my weapons (as the Chaplain was not allowed to carry a weapon in his position). We would pass (in the middle of nowhere) camels and a few Bedouins, goats, and goat herders and now and then a little oasis. I could see then how excited a foot traveler would be when he would happen upon this paradise in the middle of nothing but sand.

The Chaplain and I would arrive in one of these allied locations (which always moved – that's why we needed the radio and GPS). The Chaplain would set up and say the Mass or perform the service for our communication troops under a tent since Christian services were not allowed in that Muslin country. We had to hide the service from any possible surveillance from the Saudi's. I would stay outside and talk (or try to) with the Allied troops. This was funny as I didn't speak Arabic or French and they didn't speak English. I remember once in the Moroccan camp they handed me a hot "coke." They thought I would just love it since it was American. I graciously accepted it and thanked them by putting my right hand to my heart. They had even brought a brick oven out there in the desert to bake bread. They let me eat with them one time. Bread and hot sweet tea. It was quite a treat. I remember once on

Thanksgiving one of the communications guy's Mom had sent him a care package and it had a giant can of beans and some juice boxes. Well, he shared it with us, so we were able to get a change from our usual MREs (meals ready to eat). MREs are sealed packages of dehydrated meals (I think they have a shelf life of 20 years or so).  I heard the guys back at the base were having nice Turkey dinners, we were having beans. As a young man, it didn't matter, because I was on the adventure of my life.  I could eat turkey some other day.

Here is the most fantastic part of this story.

The Chaplain and I were always in the desert, but we got to drive back to the base every couple of weeks to clean our clothes and get a couple of good meals before we were out on the adventure again. I walked down to the laundry building and put my clothes in the washer. A guy walked in and said "Tim." I looked and it was my brother Mike! I was in shock! How is my brother in the same building as me, in a war zone, on the other side of the world and how did he find me? The window (and nobody knew this window as the Chaplain and I just "winged" our plans each day) was so tiny for me to be at that base, on that day, in that laundry room. At that time that it seemed to be a miracle. We were so happy and ran to each other and embraced.  I was never so happy to see my brother in this crazy time and place. We hung out for quite a few hours.  I remember we went to where they were selling entire chickens (roasted) and we bought one each and ate both birds. We finally finished our time together and Mike headed out with his Chaplain back to the Tank Company's next mission. I'm sure my Chaplain and I headed back out the next day.

We were there for many months and saw and did things we will never forget, but the highlight of the entire War for me was the almost impossible meeting with my brother in that tiny crack of time. Now when I think back about this meeting, I know God had his hand in it.

## Chapter 15

### Triathlete - Terry

When I was around 35 years old, I decided that I would learn how to do a triathlon. What an adventure that was especially since I had no background in long-distance swimming or biking. I signed up for a little beginner race and started swimming laps at the gym. At first, I could only swim a couple of laps. I practiced for weeks and rode my bike and ran on the treadmill. On the day of my first triathlon, I arrived at the lake. There must have been over 100 athletes or so. There was a roped-off section at the race for the transition. This is where you set up your bike and shoes for the run. I tried to copy everyone as I didn't know anyone personally that had ever participated in a triathlon. I believed that I was ready, so I walked over to the edge of the lake for the swim portion of the race to start. I was so nervous, but I went for it and to my surprise I enjoyed it. All those hours swimming laps paid off as I completed the swim without any problems. The bike ride and run also went well. I found a new passion for the sport and I was hooked.

I completed approximately 50 triathlons when at age 40 I decided I would sign up for the escape from Alcatraz triathlon in San Francisco. Again, I did not know anyone that had raced in this event, but I relished in the challenge of this event. I trained for this swim by swimming in the coldest river water I could find and I would sit in a place at the gym called the "cold plunge" for up to 5 minutes at a time to try to acclimate to the cold water assuming that it would replicate the water of the San Francisco Bay. I knew this would be the race of my triathlon career so I put in the work training as hard as I could. This race required a one and a half-mile swim from Alcatraz to Fisherman's Wharf fighting the current and choppy water, followed by a 24-mile bike ride through the Presidio area of San Francisco, then an eight-mile run down Baker Beach and then back up the notorious 400 sand steps and on to the finish. As I headed out with hundreds of other competitors on the ferry boat to go out to the starting point at Alcatraz Island I was overwhelmed with emotion. I had the feeling that I might be going out to try something beyond my abilities due to the lack of experience with such a big ocean swim. To my relief, after a tough one hour plus swim, I made it to shore and went on to complete the bike and run portions and finished strong. I had risen to the challenge and succeeded.

I did the Alcatraz swim two more times and had the great privilege of swimming the last time with my brother Tim. After a few more years I gave up triathlon and moved onto long-distance cycling. But I will never forget the awesome adventures I enjoyed racing triathlon events.

## Chapter 16

### Learning To Swim - Pat

As number four of six brothers, I was the token middle child, wanting to be noticed at the same time wanting anything but to be noticed. I desired peace, unity, and tranquility.

As I recall, not sure if I was 6, or 7, or 8, or even 9 years of age, on this vacation, we took our usual and arbitrary overnight trip to Santa Cruz for our annual summer family vacation.

To the best of my recollection, the highlights of the annual trip were that we stopped at the Nut Tree where we bought dozens of inexpensive hand-size bread loaves and each of us could have a bread loaf for ourselves as well as an individual small plate of fudge (Probably 2 ½ piece size). There was something special about this gift and opportunity that was unique to the trip. This was a city-like treat not found in the rural country town that we were being raised in.

I also recall arriving in the town proper of Santa Cruz and as soon as we settled into the low-end hotel, we made our way to the carnival-style bumper cars. This was something so unfamiliar to me, but so exciting. I had no idea what the cost must have been, and I am sure we had just one turn at the experience, but it was wonderful. I was able to speed to such exhilarating speeds and bump my elder brothers with such force, assured at least in my mind to be an impressionable impact. I loved it.

After the bumper car experience, I recall going to the miniature golf course. Please note, at the time, miniature golf courses were not a dime a dozen experience, and each hole was an adventure. I am not sure how long the 9+ holes might have taken to complete, but it has left a lasting impression in my mind. Any time I could outdo one of my elder brothers it gave me a sense of worth, and if I could ever outdo my humble father, the god-like man, I would be internally and eternally transformed. The miniature golf experience was fun but was also formative in so many ways.

This now leads to the swimming pool. As an external spectator, it probably would not resonate with much substantial worth. Yet, as a small boy only familiar with the Olivehurst Public swimming pool, and the designated rope and buoys that separated the 3-foot area from the deeper swimmer area, my experience was much different. All my brothers were swimming and having fun in the Holiday Inn pool. I joined them while entering from the shallow end as my parents watched from above on the second-floor balcony where our room was located. I walked-swam away from the entrance stairs into the pool feeling quite secure with my brothers so close for protection. To my fault, I did not notice that there wasn't a separating rope, like the home-town pool, safely separating the deep pool area from the shallow. Unknowingly I proceeded into the deep area and before I knew it, I was in territory much beyond my swimming capabilities. I could not swim. I began to gasp for air as I could not touch the bottom. There was no time to yell for help. I was already in a dire circumstance. I did not doubt that my mom and dad could see my dilemma, but they were miles away on the second floor. I panicked and slapped at the water. I had a sense I was going to die. Life became a blur. Where were my brothers? I knew they were just yards away, but they were unaware of my circumstance. I was about to die! I was going to drown!

Somehow, I must have slapped and paddled toward the edge of the pool, and eventually, I grabbed and reached the safety and security of a wall. I survived. I was alive.

I am not sure what happened, but in that dire instant, I learned to swim.

Lesson learned – We don't always feel prepared, or even know what life will reveal to us, yet, we will not only survive but will realize abilities we never knew we possessed.

## <u>Chapter 17</u>

## My Struggle / My Cross – Mike

I have been dealing with health problems for the last few years and it has increased a lot in the last year. I have been hospitalized several times. I have Diabetes and Gastroparesis. If you don't know what Gastroparesis is, I will try to explain. It is a condition that affects the stomach muscles and prevents proper stomach emptying. Gastroparesis can affect digestion. The cause might be damage to a nerve that controls stomach muscles. My body doesn't digest food like most people. The food just sits there and rots. It only releases itself by vomiting and chronic diarrhea. The pain is so bad that it's almost intolerable.

I have lost so much weight from being sick. I went from my heaviest (298 pounds) to my current weight (150 pounds). I have almost no energy and I get worn out just doing simple tasks. My doctors have just informed me that my kidney function is at 20% and I will need to go on dialysis soon. This is very scary since life expectancy on dialysis is 5-10 years! I don't want to die! Whenever the pain gets bad, I think of my Mom. She endured so much pain in her final years, yet she never complained and just put it all in God's hands! She was a true warrior!

Being sick has made me step back and look at my life. I now value the things that I took for granted. My family means so much to me. I love my wife, kids, and brothers (and their families) so much. I don't want to die! I have way too many things I still want to do! I admit that I'm scared as hell! With the support of family and friends, I'm encouraged and motivated to live a long time!

I don't know what the future holds for me or how much time I have left. I want to see my kids walk down the aisle. I want to play with grandkids, etc. I pray that God will watch over me and give me a long life!

## <u>Chapter 18</u>

### Growing Up The Youngest - Dan

Growing up as the youngest of six boys was and still is something that I treasure. Having a close-knit family is something that I will never take for granted.

I am thankful that, as I approach my 50th birthday, all of us are still together on this earth. I can't imagine the thought of not having the Kearns 6 anymore.

As I sit and ponder about each one of my brothers, I am filled with admiration and thanks. Each one of them is just a great individual. Truly kind people to the core. All so funny as well. Each has played a different role in my life.

Mike is the closest to me in age. We practically grew up together with many of the same friends. I always thought, how cool it was that Mike would allow me to hang out with his group of friends. They were all 2-3 years older than I, but I always felt accepted. To this day, Mike can make me laugh like no other. Funnier than can be. We have so many crazy memories together. Some are things that only him and I would remember or understand.

My brother Pat is someone from whom I learned to take the belief that everything will work out. His depth of spirituality and belief are second to none in my book. When our Mother was nearing the end of her life, I was able to take some comfort knowing that she was going to a better place. I never would have been able to accept it in that way without his guidance and support. I love that Pat is not afraid to take a leap of faith where others would not.

Terry is a brother that has a great love for life. Some of my best memories are just sitting around laughing with Terry and his humor. Nobody can take someone's story and make it bigger and better than Terry can. He takes a normal or mundane story or memory and brings it to life. You leave with a smile on your face after being around him.

My brother Tim is one of the most caring people I know. He always makes sure everybody is doing okay or taken care of. What a truly talented person. He can do and accomplish whatever he puts his mind to. Not to mention how athletic he is. He's the brother that I remember playing sports with for hours at a time. Basketball, tennis, playing catch, etc. I'm so grateful for those memories that we continue to make to this day.

Kevin is my eldest brother. He is also the most fearless. I am amazed at all the things he has tried or did. Jumping out of planes, hang gliding, getting his pilot's license, and flying. There are too many things to list. The part of Kevin that I admire the most though, is his true love of Family. He has always made sure that the brothers keep close and don't lose touch with one another. That family is and always will be something to treasure.

I am a better person because of these 5!!

## Chapter 19

## God's Path Is Often A Twisted Road – Kevin

If you would have asked me early on what I wanted to be when I grew up, I probably would have said a doctor. That would have made my parents proud for sure. And the alternative parent pleasing answer would have been a Priest, but at that age, I didn't think that was in the cards. I might have also wished to be a pro athlete, but even then I think I was pretty clear on my limitations.

Life played out, as it always does, and eventually, I found myself in college and had to declare a major. Somehow, I made it through the years and still wanted to be a doctor, so I chose Biology as my major, chemical science as my minor, and trusted this would provide a solid path to medical school. I completed my college education and even included a stint at the National Institute of Health doing cancer research, which would hopefully help my entre into a medical school somewhere. My plan was taking shape. Underscore "my plan" though, since it would not be long before God would make it clear He had another path in mind.

My girlfriend for the last two years of college attended school intending to obtain a "Mrs." degree. I was completely unaware of that motivation until near the end of my term, and when I hesitated to commit, ok refused to commit, she ended our relationship, left school, and returned home to the San Francisco Bay Area. In hindsight, I should have left her decision alone, completed my schooling, and tried to attend medical school as planned. But whether I thought we were "meant to be" or it was more my ego not being able to handle the rejection, I decided to put Med School on hold "briefly", and find a job close to her to win her back. Emporium Capwell, a large retail store back then, had a management training program that would guarantee I would be located near San Francisco, so this was going to be the perfect solution to my challenge. I was sure I only needed to be near her consistently for a few weeks and I would salvage my relationship and be able to return to my medical plans.

Once again, "my plan" and God's plan were a bit askew, and guess which one won out. As life would have it, I took the job at Emporium Capwell and never saw my girlfriend again. But for the first time in many years, I was experiencing life without homework and decided to enjoy a little longer. This went on for three years. I did reach a point that I felt a little guilty not making use of my science degree, but rather than try to return to the Med school path, I knew I was no longer disciplined enough to make it through, I decided to take a job selling surgical lasers and microscopes for Zeiss. Yes, I was quite qualified to handle the Science aspect. But no, I was anything but qualified or disciplined to handle the outside sales component. My territory was large, and my customers were nurses and Doctors. Who knew they liked to be entertained so much and I did have an expense account. But after a full year in the position, I had not made a single sale, so it was time to find a different calling.

I had always wanted to fly planes, so it only made sense to try and join the Navy as a fighter pilot. Low and behold, I got accepted to the Navy's flight program, AOCS, so I packed my bags and prepared to commit at least the next 7 years of my life to this latest pursuit. Off I went to Pensacola, Florida. My plan was taking shape, or so I thought. God had a different plan though, and a week later I was back home and out of the Navy. That's a story for another time, but this did start a journey that wouldn't make sense until many years later.

Unprepared to be home. Having thought my next several years were planned out, I tried several endeavors. I sold insurance benefit packages, well, tried to sell, I wasn't any good at it. I did have a job working for the 7-11 Corporation and that was ok for a couple of years, but then decided to give sales a try again and was allured by the temptation of making big money in commercial real estate. Alas, it was clear now that I did not possess the sales gene. What I was beginning to see though, was just how important relationships were in business and in life. My commercial broker job didn't pan out, but along the way, I would meet people who would help me in surprising ways. One was a property manager, who I got along quite well with, and who also was married to someone I had worked with at 7-11.

God's dominos were beginning to line up, although it would still be quite some time before His game would be revealed. I knew I could no longer survive the commercial real estate gig, as it was, I had made no money in over a year and only survived by supplementing with a nighttime waiter income. I reached out to my property manager friend to ask for a job and was told that although she liked me, having no direct experience would make my hire a very long shot. A bit disappointed, I decided to take a break, obtain a passport, and go visit my brother Tim who was stationed in Okinawa. At this point I had nothing to lose and no compelling options, so what the heck. The day before I was to depart, I got a call from my property management friend. She shared that this never happens, but an opportunity came up for an entry-level assistant manager position on one of her properties. The open opportunity sure not to last, so I needed to interview quickly. I told her I was leaving for Okinawa the next day, so it had to be that day and somehow, she was able to schedule an interview with the hiring manager. I threw on the only tie I owned and dashed to the interview. It didn't last long and although I thought we got along well, I certainly wasn't overconfident I would be chosen, and I had a plane to catch anyway. So off I went, unemployed and thinking I would enjoy time with my brother and then figure things out when I returned.

After two weeks in Okinawa, also a story for another time, I returned and fully prepared to start from scratch and try to figure out a new path. Long before voice mail, I checked my answering machine when I got home and shockingly listened as my friend told me they wanted to hire me for the assistant manager position. Holy moly, what a shock, what a relief, and little did I know, what an opportunity that would be a stepping stone to something much bigger.

I spent the next decade learning the commercial real estate business. I enjoyed the work, but it was the relationships that I formed along the way that would make a difference. I was working as a "landlord" and one of the commercial brokers that I used as a partner to help lease office space, decided to leave the business. Unlike me, he was very successful, so deciding to leave was surprising. But he ended up at a little startup company called eBay as their marketing director. As they grew, they decided they needed to hire a real estate manager and since my former broker was the only one who had any real estate experience, they turned to him for a suggested candidate. We had always got along well, so he threw my name into the mix. Even though I had no corporate real estate experience, because of his recommendation, I was offered an interview. Not sure if it was because of his reference, my fudging a bit on my experience, divine intervention, or a combination of all, somehow, I was offered the job. A job that would become a career, a career that would span over two decades, take me to over 40 countries, and more importantly, put me in a position to help so many people. Working for a tech company meant the salary would be ok, but it also came with stock options. These would prove quite valuable, especially when associated with a company on an insane growth curve. Far from "rich", but the added income would allow for much sharing and good to be done. Helping to resurrect a Catholic church that was struggling, funding many charitable endeavors, and most importantly, being there to help my brothers when needed. Truly a blessing from God. A blessing for which I am daily, eternally grateful.

A long, twisted path no one could have ever seen coming. Well, almost no one. Trust God's plan….it always works out for the best… eventually.

## Chapter 20

## Bullies - Tim

I was a "happy go lucky" kid in elementary school. We lived in a small community where we had lots of friends that lived just a block or two away. Our school, Johnson Park Elementary was only about 1/4 of a mile from our house. I would walk to and from school with a couple of my brothers and some friends each day. Each day at school, we would play basketball, softball, or some other fun sport and everyone seemed to get along.

Well, this next event happened in either 4th or 5th grade. For some reason, this bully, Lance Baker (in the same grade as me) started picking on some of the smaller kids. Pushing them down, calling them names, etc. He started to attract a following of impressionable kids (boys and girls) that would follow him around and laugh when he would torment these smaller children. He was one of the bigger kids in school. I was about the same height, but much skinnier. Well,

I watched this a time or two until I just had to say something.  I told him to stop doing that and he turned on me.  I was athletic, but by no means had ever been in a fight.  He came at me and shouted, "What are YOU going to do about it?"  We exchanged a few words and his "followers" were oohing and aahing about the confrontation.  I don't know where this came from, but I just closed my eyes and swung as hard as I could and "blam" right in the kisser.  He fell and started crying.  This happened right after school let out and it was so funny how his "followers" abandoned him and started following me home.  How wishy-washy they were (just like Democrats) :)

The next day, Lance came up to me and started talking to me like we were best friends, and like nothing had happened.  He stopped harassing the kids and for a couple of years, he and I did become best friends.

A couple of years later, the shoe was on the other foot.  Lance was not involved, but my older brother Kevin was.  I was being a little smartass to my brother when my Mom or Dad was around.  I would tease Kev and then run and yell for my Mom and say Kevin is trying to hit me or torture me.  This would go on day after day, until ... the one fateful day this routine was going on just at the time my Dad pulled in from work.  I must have yelled for him, Dad, Dad, Kev is trying to hit me.  He was tired of it and said OK, you two go in the yard and have it out.  I got all brave and puffed out my chest and thought ... I will show him a thing or two.  Well, we squared up and started dancing around as boxers do and I may have swung a time or two, not hitting Kev at all and he swung only one punch, connecting right square in the middle of my nose.  I fell and laid there for a couple of minutes and once I got up, never teased Kev again :)

## Chapter 21

## The Minesweeper – Terry

I joined the Navy in 1983 on the buddy program with my brother Tim. We left that summer for Boot Camp in Orlando Florida. After graduating eight weeks later we both received orders for (A) school in Meridian, Mississippi for approximately six weeks then my solo adventure began. While Tim received orders to the USS Kittyhawk CV 63 an aircraft carrier otherwise referred to as a floating city with thousands of shipmates, I on the other hand received orders to the USS Conquest MSO 488 a wooden minesweeper with a crew of 49 shipmates. My ship was so small that you were sure to get seasick every time we went out to sea for the first few months.

Our ship got tossed around so bad that you would not be allowed outside and you had to seatbelt yourself into your rack when you tried to sleep. I was assigned to a top bunk that had such little room above me that I had to slide out of the rack to turn over. Talk about claustrophobic situations. The ship would rock and roll with the wood creaking all night and we would tip over so far that I would be praying for the ship to not flip over in the middle of the ocean.

Eating chow in our galley was another interesting challenge as our chairs were not fixed to the floor. Our food trays would stay on the table but when the ship would roll with a big wave we would all slide to the wall and have to wait for the rollback to slide back to our plates to take a bite.

I lived on that ship for 2 1/2 years but like everything else in life you learn to adapt and after the first six months I would never get seasick anymore and learned to be proud of that ship and the work we were doing. I will always be proud of having such a unique experience.

## <u>Chapter 22</u>

### The Top Drawer - Pat

I didn't realize it at the time, but as many years and as life has gone by, I have learned more and more by the life example that my father had taught me.

My father lived a very humble and simple life. He was an educated man with a master's degree which at the time was not a dime a dozen, it meant something. He was also a teacher. Not a professor, but a middle school teacher. You know, those teachers who really teach. He didn't earn a high salary, but it was steady and was enough with a second job teaching night school that he provided the basics for a wife and six sons.

I can remember two things he enjoyed and valued as a possession. He liked his tools and for a short time liked his very inexpensive Gregor fishing boat and 7.5 hp air-cooled outboard motor. He dreamed one day he could get one of those more expensive water-cooled boat motors, maybe even a 15 hp but also realized that it might never happen. The Gregor galvanized fishing boat was nothing special, just a basic bottom of the line used boat with three small bench seats, a fishing boat that could hold up to three people. I am sure he didn't pay more than a few hundred dollars for it.

I don't recall my dad owning that boat for too many years. I assume he eventually needed to sell it to make ends meet. As for his tools, he only bought craftsman tools because they were guaranteed for life, yet having six sons who didn't have the same respect for tools, they were often lost of indefinitely displaced somewhere.

However, my dad did have the top drawer of his dresser in my parents' bedroom. Not the dresser that he shared with my mother, but the small upright dresser that held his socks and underwear. The top drawer, however, only held miscellaneous personal items. No one would ever dare to take anything from that drawer. Never spoken, but we all understood that the drawer was the only thing that was hands-off to others in his life.

I can only assume that my brothers did what I had done. We had to see what my father kept in that drawer. I recall one day peeking in that drawer to see what my dad kept as his most special items. What was it that he had accumulated over a lifetime, and didn't want to share it with anyone else? Finally, sneaking into the room one day when my parents were out, I saw upon opening the top drawer: a pocketknife, a rosary, a few Irish buttons such as "Kiss me I'm Irish" and what appeared to be a few keepsake items given to him as gifts from students. He had a variety of handkerchiefs with the Letters TK (For Thomas Kearns) embroidered on them, an inexpensive compass, and a few tie clips. That was it.

My father sacrificed his entire life, working two jobs, to provide for his family and possessed such selflessness that all he protected as special keepsakes were the accumulation of items that could not have accounted for a worth of greater than ten dollars.

As I reflect on my father's simplicity, sacrifice, and selflessness, I am hit square-faced with my gluttony of thought and action.

Thank you, Dad, for still teaching me today from your life example. Things have no worth. Character and honorable action, especially humble, non-public, sacrificial action is invaluable.

## Chapter 23

### Blessing In Disguise - Mike

I suffer from Type 2 Diabetes and Gastroparesis (delayed stomach emptying) which is the most painful thing I've ever experienced! It feels like you're being punched in the stomach over and over again! I also had my right leg amputated because of Diabetes in 2012. I walk with a prosthetic leg which has kept me out of a wheelchair.

I was thinking about this the other day... I was pretty wild growing up and had a bad drinking problem. I would drink an 18 pack of beer every day and even more on the weekends. I smoked a pack and a half of cigarettes a day and was in bad shape. Let's look at this. That's 30 days x 18 beers a day, which equals 540 beers a month and 30 cigs x 30 days equals 900 cigs a month. EVERY MONTH! This went on for years! I don't know how I managed to stay out of jail! Joining the Navy and leaving town was the only thing that kept me out. I did my share of partying while in the Navy but managed to stay out of trouble just enough to stay out of jail.

Having been diagnosed with Diabetes saved my life. Had I kept up the drinking and smoking, I know I would have died by now at the rate I was going! In 2012 I gave up drinking and smoking (Cold Turkey) and even though I suffer from medical Issues... I AM STILL HERE! I can't count the number of times I've been to the E.R. because of my diabetes and gastroparesis. There is no cure! I've gone from my highest weight (298 lbs.) to my now lowest (146 lbs.) and I fight to try and put on weight daily. The depression gets so bad sometimes that I fall into a "Funk!" I thank God for my wife! I would not be here if it wasn't for her! She takes such awesome care of me. I'm blessed to have the support of my family as well. The prayers are so appreciated and needed! Prayer plays such a big part in my daily struggles. When I'm going through "Bad Times" and the pain is so bad, I just keep telling myself that God doesn't give us more than we can handle and I fight my way through it! God has NEVER let me down or given me more than I could handle!

I'm not sure what the future has in store for me but I will continue to fight every day!  I have so much love for my family. My Brothers mean everything to me and I'm proud to be 1/6 of the Kearns Boyz!

## <u>Chapter 24</u>

## The Girl Who Stole My Heart Forever - Dan

The day that my daughter entered this world, was the day my life would change forever. Contrary to most during the '90s, we didn't want to know the gender ahead of time. I never understood why you would want the element of surprise taken away from you. Especially the miracle of life.

When Kaylynn was born, the nurse asked us what name would be given to this wonderful creation. We gave her the name, and with the assistance of the nurse, determined the spelling.

This wasn't my first crack at parenthood though. I became an instant father of an eleven-year-old girl and an eight-your-old son when I married. They were good kids though, and well on their way in life. This was a bit different as you can imagine. Kaylynn was so little and didn't walk or talk. Didn't do much at all. I was out of my element for sure. How do I know if she's okay or if she needed something? To make matters even more stressful, Kaylynn was prone to seizures in her first few years. To the point where she stopped breathing a few times. More than once, I thought I would lose her.

Kaylynn would become my world. My little buddy. We would do everything together. We had a home on 2.5 acres with a creek running through it. Kaylynn and I would play for hours. I taught her that it was okay to squat behind the tree when you have to go pee. You don't want to have to run back to the house and ruin our fun. Keep in mind, I grew up with all boys. I didn't know how to raise a girl. That was her mom's responsibility to teach her the "girly" things in life.

We had many wonderful and crazy experiences. Kaylynn never lets me forget that I talked her into jumping onto the "water blob" when she was about 6. This was probably a 15 x 15 flotation device that some camps have floating in the lake. You walk up a 15-foot ladder, walk to the edge of the platform, and jump down on it. Then you crawl to the edge of it, and the next person jumps onto it and catapults the person on the end, high into the air. Kaylynn didn't want to do it, but I encouraged her anyway. I wanted to launch her. We never got that far. She reluctantly walked up the ladder ahead of me and jumped off. She was so light, that she bounced off of it and landed in the nearby shallow water. She thought she broke her back. Thankfully a doctor was on sight to ease our worries. She would be okay.

I remember taking her on jet skis full throttle. Going on four-wheelers as fast as we can go up on the levees. Kaylynn and

I would have many adventures together that would sometimes end with us rushing to the emergency room, where she would ultimately receive stitches.

My life revolved around her. It would crush me when she would come home from school sometimes in tears. Girls were being mean to her. Or when a relationship with a guy would end abruptly.

All I wanted to do was put joy into this little girl's life. I loved going to the father/daughter dances together when she was younger. Dropping her off at school. Going to her basketball and soccer games. Watching her play tennis in high school. I wouldn't miss a match. Coaching her little league teams. So many incredible memories.

She's grown into an amazing woman now. She excels in school. In the process of getting her Master's degree. She's given me the most incredible granddaughter, Addison. She's a loving wife. She couldn't have picked a better man in Ryan. Last but not least, she loves her Dad. I couldn't be prouder of her.

## <u>Chapter 25</u>

## I Wish I Would Have Known My Brothers Better - Kevin

Growing up I can't recall a time my brothers and I weren't together. I am the oldest of 6 boys, so mom and dad creating all 6 of us didn't happen overnight. I vaguely remember times in the very early days when we had only the beginnings of the family, memories most likely strengthened by the photos I am so lucky to have from those days more than five decades ago. Although it is a bit of a blur, I distinctly remember occasions when "the family" was together, just not crystal clear how many brothers were involved each time.

Tim, being brother #2, is relevant in most of my early recollections. Makes sense since I ruled my childhood world being the only child until he invaded my paradise. And then they just kept coming. Being Catholic, mom and dad felt compelled to build a family and in less than 12 years, I had 5 younger brothers.

My brothers as adults are not nearly as mysterious to me as their childhood selves. In these later years, we have done a better job connecting, and surprise some people with how close we have remained over time. It is through this evolving connecting that I have learned that I had some pretty amazing younger brothers growing up, but seems I missed a good portion of the journey. And honestly, I don't know why. When I think back to those times, nothing jumps out as a compelling reason. I don't remember deciding my life didn't have time for my brothers. So how did I miss my youngest brother pitching no-hitters or winning MVP of basketball tournaments. All 5'3" of him…. How did I miss my brother Mike diving off the starting block of a swimming sprint in his speedo… Tim and Terry excelling at multiple sports….and I would have loved to watch Pat wrestle. It's like they had entire childhoods that I missed, but I don't think I was gone, so not sure how that happened. I try not to regret much in life. Learn from mistakes, try to do better, but if you can't change something, not much use lamenting about it. But I do regret missing my brothers growing up.

I, like anyone else, don't know when my last day on this earth will be, but I am confident I am closer to that day than to the day I was born. Otherwise, I would have to live past 120, and that doesn't seem a part of God's script for my life story. As a result, I am much more conscious of my mortality these days. One question I have been asking myself lately is if I knew the actual day that any one of my brothers would die, and certainly if it was anytime soon, would I treat them any different than I do now? Would I spend more time with them? Would I talk to them in ways or about topics that we avoid now? When I catch myself thinking that I have time, time to make up for missed opportunities, time to catch up "later", all I need to do is think about my time with my dad. It has been a hard lesson to learn about the risk of putting conversations and "moments" off to a time in the future that never comes. I waited too late with my dad. I never expected him to die suddenly, thinking I had several more years with him, and I have regretted it ever since. I need to do better with my brothers. I don't want to miss any more of them "growing up". They are all a blessing from God in my life and I need to treat them accordingly.

I want to know them better. And I know I only have today.

## <u>Chapter 26</u>

## Harley – Tim

One of the greatest treasures God has ever blessed me with was when he brought our little Harley Brian into our life.  I have many loves in my life, my wife, our boys, my brothers, my parents, my sister (will meet her for the first time in heaven) nieces, nephews, and even my brother's horses (those will be in a different story), but little Harley has extraordinarily captured my heart.  Harley (middle name Brian) is a one-year-old Maltese Poodle mix (Maltipoo).  He is a tiny little thing only weighing 8 lbs.  He is very athletic, and my wife has taught him quite a few tricks.  When we first brought Harley home, at 10 weeks old, he seemed so small at 2 ½ pounds.  We were scared he would injure himself if he fell off the couch.  Well, those times have changed as he leaps up on the couch now with no problem and can jump/fly off it at a gallop.  The way he looks in your eyes with such a locked-on stare melts my heart.  He is so happy to see me when I get home.  You can count on, every time, his tail will be wagging 100 miles an hour and he will be jumping and spinning with excitement.  This will immediately quell any frustration that the day has brought up to this point.  Sometimes, I will lay on the bed or the couch and be checking email on my phone.  He will leap up and jump up on my chest and duck his head under my phone and between it and my eyes.  He will then lay down staring at me for attention.  It is the most precious thing ever.  I think everyone should have a dog in their life.  It is such a special bond to love and be loved so unconditionally.  Dogs are indisputably one of God's crowing achievements.

## Chapter 27

### Trust In God's Plan – Terry

Three years ago, I ended my 30-year career of working in the home medical health field. I knew everything about this industry as I had worked my way up from the delivery driver to the director position at the hospital. I had planned on working there until retirement. Well, I believe God had another plan for me.

All of a sudden without notice the CEO of the hospital called all of us to a meeting to let us know they were no longer going to have our department and we were laid off. 67 people lost their jobs that day. While others were in shock and panic, I believed that this was God's way of steering my path in another direction.

So right away I decided that commercial truck driving seemed like a good adventure. So, I enrolled in a truck driving school and earned my class A driving license. I started driving the big double bottom gravel trucks which I enjoyed. Then I moved onto the big 53-foot trailers hauling carpet. But now I drive a propane truck and fill propane tanks at residential properties. It is with this job that I get to meet so many people and let God's light shine through me.

This job is an absolute blessing for me and all because I believed God had a plan for my life and I just needed to trust in Him. God will always provide if you love and believe in Him.

## Chapter 28

### Fourth Of July - Pat

I have such fond memories of the Fourth of July on Jeffery Court. First of all, I would like to mention that we did not have much money growing up. Dad was a school teacher with six sons, and mom was a homemaker. Yet, Dad found a way each year to buy a box of fireworks for the family. I am pretty sure that it was the cheapest box available, but it was a box of fireworks. It contained a few fountain cones, sparklers, black grow worms, spinners, and more. Dad was in charge of the box, and depending on our age we might have even been able to light a few of the items. I delightfully remember the sparklers. Lighting them and then running around waving the sparkler in the air and creating such illuminating designs.

Even though we didn't have much to offer in means of material goods (i.e. quantity and quality of fireworks) our house still seemed to draw the other kids from the court. I am pretty sure the draw was not the size of our firework box, but a chance to join in and participate with a cohesive family with a mom, dad, and children all working together and without complaint, enjoying the simplicity of sharing time together, rejoicing in the beauty of the sparklers, erupting cones, and spinning objects. Everyone was always welcome at our home, and welcome at the edge of the driveway especially when darkness arrived on the fourth.

Looking back, I can see that my parents went to great effort to ensure that we participated in the customs on the time even if it were a scaled-down version of what others might have experienced. Yet, we never knew that what we were doing might not be as elaborate as some of the other family celebrations. The important fact was that we were doing it together and having fun together.

As I reflect on these memories, I continue to gain insight into the wisdom of my parents. They never complained as to our financial status, our ability to keep up with the Jones' of the world, or even those all-too-common temporary setbacks. They just continued day in and day out to try to be happy, to be thankful, and to provide to the best of their ability for their children. Perseverance, tradition, unity, family, thankfulness, simplicity, and effort come to mind from this experience.

## Chapter 29

### Faith - Mike

It's funny how we think we are invincible, especially where our health is concerned. I've always been pretty active. I played sports (although not too good) all my life. Having Diabetes and especially Gastroparesis just drains me of all my energy. Flare upsets come out of nowhere and they have hospitalized me many times in the last few years. I HATE THE HOSPITAL!

I've dealt with so much pain because of these diseases. I just found out I only have 20% kidney function left and soon will be doing Dialysis. I'm scared! I find myself praying a lot! I know God only gives us as much as we can tolerate but it seems so overwhelming at times! I know my Mom and Dad are watching over me from Heaven.

I'm so blessed to be married to my wife, Lisa! She is a Saint! She takes such awesome care of me and makes sure I'm doing all that I'm supposed to do. She has sacrificed so much for me that without her I would not be around! She gave me two great kids who would do anything for anybody! I'm truly blessed!

I am not sure what the future holds but I know if I trust in God, things will work out in the end!

## Chapter 30

## A Second Chance - Dan

Funny where life takes you sometimes. I was married for nearly 20 years. When that relationship ending, I was sure that I would never marry again. Heck, we were raised that you only marry once, and that's for life.

What was that next chapter of my life going to look like? The kids were raised. I was on my own. All I knew for sure is that God will have a hand in it.

Maybe this was my chance to explore and do things I always wanted to do. I did that for a while. I would go on hikes to amazing waterfalls. Go on long but satisfying bike rides. Experience road trips to take in the beautiful scenery. The problem was, there was nobody to do it with. Sure, once in a while there was a friend or family member to join me, but they had their regular lives and families already.

I didn't know the first thing about dating. I looked at a couple of those dating sites but that wasn't for me. I had friends try and set me up. That was a disaster. Thankfully though, I always believed that if I was meant to be in a solid relationship, it would happen when I least expected it.

That's where Barbara comes in. We knew and went to school together from the second grade through high school. I would consider us friendly with one another, but we hung out with different people and different crowds. Funny, we always liked each other but we never dated. After high school ended, I would not see or even hear of her for the next 25 years.

Fast forward to 2014. I am visiting our hometown, where my brother Mike and I were having a book signing. Barbara had just ended a relationship with her previous partner and had heard about this event taking place. When she arrived and approached a friend of mine, who I was standing right next to, I was blown away. Who is this beauty? I didn't recognize her. It had been too many years.

We were introduced and the rest is history. I've grown to love this woman like no other. She is such a positive force in my life and such a pleasant human being to be around. She makes me laugh every day. Now WE, take amazing hikes, go on adventurous bike rides, and partake on many memorable road trips. She's my best friend.

We will be married by the time you read this book.

## <u>Chapter 31</u>

**Superheroes Can Be Human Too - Kevin**

I didn't think of my parents as being any different than other parents growing up. They seemed quite normal, even ordinary at the time. We didn't have a lot of money, how could we with Dad being a school teacher and mom a homemaker, together raising six boys. But we also didn't "want" for much. We had simple lives, but they were safe and full.

Our parents weren't high school sweethearts in the typical sense. Dad was eight years older than mom, so they weren't in high school together as students. But he was her high school teacher. So, in a way, they were high school sweethearts, just a bit controversial. Over time they confirmed the pureness of their relationship though as they were each other's first and only marriage. They stayed married for over 40 years, created a beautiful family of six boys, and together overcame every challenge God placed in their path.

I was nine years old when we first discovered mom had what would one day be known as manic depression, or "bi-polar" disease. At the time we had no idea what caused her to just "go crazy" periodically, and then follow up with severe depression. The first time it happened, I remember her ending up in a mental hospital in Berkeley, complete with a padded cell and electric shock therapy. I do remember being scared, wondering if she would ever get better, and if we had lost our mom for good, but Dad never gave up hope. He loved her so deeply. Over the years we became quite familiar with the mental disease, and begrudgingly so did our neighbors. Thankfully with the advancement of medical science, she was able to keep the episodes somewhat in check. The frequency, intensity, and duration of the occurrences declined. This was over many years though, and I know it took a toll on my dad. It wasn't easy on us either, but we always had our dad to lead us, and her, out of the darkness. I don't know how he did it. How he never stopped loving her. How he never gave up, no matter how many times my mom's affliction reared its ugly head, all too often in the most inopportune times. The beast would come out of nowhere, sometimes in a very public way, totally embarrass us boys, but Dad never seemed fazed. He just loved her so much. He was such a superhero. But he was only human.

I vividly remember one time that has stuck in my memory all these years. I can see it so clearly. Mom had just finished one of her more trying episodes and my dad was just spent emotionally and physically. We were home, and although Mom was not in danger, she was still very trying. My dad had enough and just got up and left. He got into his little orange Nissan truck and drove away. I didn't realize he had left, thinking initially he had just ducked outside to have a smoke. But when he didn't come back in, I went outside to look for him and saw his truck was gone. I immediately felt fear creep over me. Dad had never done this before. Sure, times were extreme all too often and I was constantly amazed at how he had always weathered every storm, claimed that I wouldn't have blamed him if he ever threw in the towel, but always drew such comfort from the belief that he never would. Not Dad, not my superhero. Maybe he just went to the store for more cigs, surely, he would be back in a few minutes. But the minutes went by and he never returned. I don't remember how old I was at the time, I thought I was younger but I must have just turned 16 because I could drive. I needed to go find my dad. We needed him. I needed him. Fortunately, we had a second car. It was a beater car for sure, but I didn't care, it worked so I jumped in and started my search.

I don't know why, but I had a feeling I knew where he would go. In the town of Marysville, about 5 miles from our house, there was a lake called Ellis Lake. It was a place my dad would often go to think and sneak a smoke or three. It wasn't far from the mental health facility in town that he had frequented so many times over the years when mom was being treated, so I think he found peace there. At least I hoped that was where he would go because otherwise, I had no idea. And if he was there, it possibly meant he had not left for good.

Heading down D Street into town, just before turning left to go over the 10th Street Bridge, one can turn right onto 9th street and head to the south end of the lake. It's a manmade lake with an easy walk surrounding the perimeter and benches placed randomly all along the way. I prayed I would see his truck parked somewhere and then would look for the closest bench. As I made the turn, the image that is forever baked into my mind's eye is one of what looked like a very frail, very old man hobbling across the street. He was aware of oncoming traffic so he was trying to run to get out of the way, but he could only go so fast. I felt sorry for the man. Then I realized the old man was my old man! Being my superhero, my mental image of him was always this larger than life, strong, capable, man. But here he was, clearly hampered physically, far from super. I quickly parked and ran back to where I hoped he would be. I was both relieved to find him on a nearby bench, but simultaneously so scared that he would tell me he wasn't coming back home. Although probably justifiable, God knows what he had endured for so many years, but there was no way we could make it without him. I sat next to him and meekly said hi. He looked so tired, I started to cry. I asked him if he was ok, and he genuinely seemed surprised that I was upset. He asked me why and I shared that I was scared that he was leaving us. Now my dad was not an overtly physically affectionate person. He loved us deeply, but it was more of a love that we just knew, not one that was often affirmed with physical gestures. But he knew how frightened I was and he turned to me, putting his hand on my shoulder. It was trembling, I remember that. He looked me in the eye and said "Son, I could never leave your mom or my boys. I just needed a break for a little bit, but I will be home soon". I asked him to promise he would come home and he just nodded, but I believed him. He asked me to go back home to take care of mom, and he would see me in a little while. I drove home and about an hour later, he pulled into the driveway as well. Dad never did that again.

Today, whenever I am back in Maryville and drive past that lake, my memory returns to that evening. I see my dad running across the street and I am sad when I think of the pain he was experiencing. But at the same time, I am filled with thankfulness for the blessing he truly was. He will forever be my superhero. Human, but super all the same.

## <u>Chapter 32</u>

### Perseverance

My wife Angela and I love to hike.  We have been hiking for many years and love to explore new places.  We just happen to live only 3 hours from one of the most spectacular hiking environments in the world.  Yosemite.  This is home to Half Dome, El Capitan, Upper and Lower Yosemite Falls, Glacier Point, etc.  We have been blessed to be able to hike many of these and although extremely challenging, we have been successful in completing many of them.

On one of the hikes, Upper Yosemite, we started early in the morning as we usually do.  We both had packs filled with food, water, ropes, first aid kit, etc. weighing only about 20 lbs.  We were used to hiking with this amount of weight and after eating a bagel, we headed up the trail.  The first mile consisted of a 1000-foot climb and some of the trail was sand.  We had been hiking on relatively flat ground leading up to this hiking trip but thought we were well prepared physically. About ½ a mile in I started to struggle. I was out of breath and my energy was zapped. The entire hike up to the stream feeding the falls was around 4 miles, so we didn't think it was going to be that difficult. After taking many breaks along the way we finally make it up to the 1-mile marker. I was lightheaded and completely exhausted. Embarrassed as I was, I had to turn around and head back down. Angela could have made the hike easily but came back down with me. I went to the doctor a few days later for a regular checkup and found out that I had diabetes. My sugar level was 400. It is supposed to be around 90. People are put into the hospital with readings this high. No wonder my energy was zapped on the hike a few days earlier. I didn't notice the lack of energy on the flat trails we did to prepare for the hike, but once I hit the inclines, my energy store ran out quickly. My doctor had me cut out sugar and most of the carbs I was eating and that did the trick. After about a month, my blood sugar level returned to normal and I again started to feel stronger. A few months later, we tried the same hike again. I was a little nervous since I did so terribly on the first try. We loaded our packs, headed out early again, and up the hill we went. We took it slow and lo and behold, we hit the first mile and felt pretty good. On to the second mile. This terrain was a little better as we ascended the side of the cliff with the waterfall constantly on our right side. The third and fourth miles were tough as we had to traverse giant boulders on the path. It was slow going, but it was worth it. Once at the top, the view was spectacular. We could see the entire Yosemite Valley from our vantage point. The way down was not much easier than the way up, as we had to traverse the giant boulders and huge declines (sometimes it is easier to climb up than down as it puts so much stress on the knees).  Anyway, once we hit the floor and we give the high fives, we could reflect on how we didn't give up on this adventure.  We failed, learned from our mistakes (corrected them), and tried again.  Don't worry about biting off more than you can chew … you eventually just might like the taste it leaves in your mouth.

## Chapter 33

### Life-Changing Events – Terry

When I look back at my life so far it is very clear to me that certain events will change your life forever. In my early years, I had a carefree attitude and was a very wild child. As I entered early adulthood, I still took many risks but mainly only worried about myself and lived a very selfish life.

Then when I was 27 years old, I met my wife Debi and my life changed forever. Through my relationship with the absolute love of my life, we had two beautiful children and along with my two stepchildren I learned to put family before myself. I became a much better version of myself while trying to be a good husband, father, provider, and role model to others. I have in return been so blessed in my life. I often wonder what my life might have been if not for the wonderful experience of meeting my wife.

## Chapter 34

## My Children: Better Than I Could Be - Pat

As a boy and as a man, I never stopped dreaming and believing that I might someday be better than I was. I often look back to my childhood and reflected on my high school days and even some of those early trials and accomplishments. At the time I just knew that I would become something great someday. Well, that day has never occurred, and now into midlife and edging toward older adulthood, I realize that greatness is not going to happen..

However, something exceptional occurs when we realize that all we had hoped to be someday has occurred in the lives of our children.

I always wanted to be something special, although at best, I had only become mediocre at most things. Yet, when my son progressed to become, even though it wasn't without disappointment and various setbacks, an elite Special Forces military man I couldn't help but be filled with pride. He wasn't just a regular Special Forces person like the SEALS, or Delta Force, or Pararescue, or Ranger, but a member of an elite group whose missions are always secret and will never be revealed by those who enact them. He travels covertly from continent to continent and does things he will never receive praise for but through his and his team's actions will save thousands of lives. He has become someone I had only dreamed of becoming and one who I could never be. He is better!

I also have daughters who possess hearts more sincere, open, and empathetic than mine could ever be. How did they surpass me in so many ways? They have a love so much deeper than I could ever feel or imagine. I would be jealous if it wasn't that my children possessed such a gift. It must be God's grace or through the example of their mother and her soul that taught them so well and shaped their being.

As I progress in age, I see ever so clearly my weakness, my failures, and my limitations. I can also see God's grace more clearly in my life and how he has saved me on so many occasions from myself, my free-will, and from all of my bad choices.

Even though I will always see my father as a man with so much more character and resolve than I will ever have, I can only imagine that at times he must have looked upon one or more of his sons as I look upon my children with such amazement of who they have become, despite who I am.

God is so wonderful and these gifts of insights and reflections enliven my soul and do more for me than anything this world can and could offer. Thank you, Lord, for the gift of children, their resilience, their fortitude, and their desire to dream and become greater than their parents.

## Chapter 35

## Faith II - Mike

My health has declined in the last few years. I'm a Type 2 Diabetic with Gastroparesis. I lost my right leg to Diabetes in 2012. It's been a struggle, to say the least. I have been hospitalized many times from complications from this killer disease. I'm down to 140 pounds, which is the lowest I have ever been. I'm getting ready to start Dialysis and it is SCARY! I don't know what to expect. All I hear is a bunch of different stories. The unknown is always scary! I'm going to be doing Dialysis at home as opposed to going into the clinic three days a week. I've read that this is a better alternative. So, we shall see?!

The one thing that has NOT changed is my Faith! Throughout all my sicknesses, I always remember the saying "God will never give you more than you can handle!" Something like that. It's true...As bad as the pain gets sometimes, I pray about it and it goes away. Sometimes it takes longer than other times but eventually, it comes and goes! Prayer is huge in my life! I'm not sure what is coming as far as my health is concerned but I do know that God has a plan for all of us and I just need to trust in Him and "Keep the faith!"

Am I afraid to die? On the one hand, I'm looking forward to seeing my parents in Heaven. Meeting my sister for the first time and seeing all the friends I have lost growing up. On the other hand, I would miss my Wife, Kids, Family, and Friends! I just need to trust in God and leave it in His hands!

## Chapter 36

### When Life Gives You Fire - Dan

Life comes at a person from all different directions and in many different forms. Some people choose to face it head-on while others may tread through it lightly. I don't think there's necessarily a wrong path to take. It all depends on the individual.  Some may choose the latter, careful not to take risks, while navigating cautiously, thinking that this will keep them safe. Others decide that the only way to live and thrive in this world is to take chances, willing to accept the consequences to get to the top of whatever they desire.

Regardless of who you are as a person, you never really know how you will react or respond when confronted with a catastrophic event. This became our reality in November 2018, when the deadliest and most destructive wildfire in California history broke out in our small town of Paradise.

In the days and weeks after losing our home and everything that we owned, Barbara and I were left to ponder what do we do now. The emptiness we felt was so strong. Your emotions go from sadness to anger, fear, and so many more. But the feeling that ultimately came flying through and saving the day was thankfulness.

We were happy to be alive. Our families offered so much emotional support over the next several months. We had friends that we hadn't seen or heard from in 25 or more years who reached out to us. Many who assisted with furniture and monetary donations. Even strangers and organizations were there to help out with numerous items, including clothing. Not to forget the first responders and community members who risked their lives to save others. We were so grateful for everyone who took their time to help others in need.

Two years later and counting, we continue to live our lives with the perspective that everything happens for a reason. We look at people differently than we may have before that day. We look at life as an opportunity to enjoy every day and share our happiness with the world. We could care less about material things because they can be taken away so quickly. But you won't take our happiness. We won't let you.

## Chapter 37

## Reality Punch - Kevin

Mike Tyson once said, "Everyone has a plan until they get punched in the mouth". He was one bad dude and he knew that many a soul could create a brave persona in their minds, but as soon as they felt the reality of a punch in the nose, they came quickly back to their mortal human self.

I don't remember how old I was exactly, I think somewhere between 8-10 years, but I do remember clearly the experience. It probably comes as no surprise that a household filled with boys would include a couple of pairs of boxing gloves. We had a space between our house and the neighbors that was probably 12 feet wide and maybe just as deep before reaching the backyard fence. One day a few of the neighborhood kids were over and we decided to have a boxing match. My dad was there and he was going to referee the matches. He paired me and another boy my age, Kenny, and instructed us we would go for one minute. I was a bit nervous since I had never really fought anyone before other than my brother, and that wasn't really fighting. And Kenny was known as a fairly quiet but tough kid in the neighborhood. We were friends, sort of, but certainly had never tested each other with our fists. Dad gave the verbal "gong" of the mythical bell, and Kenny and I started to fight. We were both a bit too selective in our punches to land many or even throw more than a few, but I recall I got a few jabs in between my overly defensive posture. The minute elapsed and dad sounded the verbal "gong" again ending the round. I was excited because I did better than I thought and even started to feel a bit cocky. When my Dad suggested the round had been a tie and we should have a second round, I jumped at the chance to display my newfound pugilistic prowess. Then my dad walked over to me and gave me some ill-fated advice. He said it was time to unleash the "windmill". Just go in there and start swinging like crazy and I was sure to dominate Kenny. I was a bit surprised that the "referee" was giving me advice against my opponent, but with my confidence brimming I thought what the heck, go for it.

Dad sounded the start of round two and I went in swinging. Forget any defense, it was time to show this neighborhood tough guy just who he was messing with. I'm not sure how many swings I actually unleashed but what I remember clearly is the smack in the nose Kenny landed on me. Just one, but that was enough, I was done. It hurt. And all my newfound confidence evaporated in an instant. Thanks for the advice, Dad.

About a decade later I was attending Chico State and memories of that punch from Kenny had long been forgotten. I was in pretty decent shape and for some reason still unknown to me, I wanted to try boxing. There was a boxing club on campus and I knew a couple of guys who spent time there and they enjoyed it. I decided to give it a shot but knew I needed to train quite a bit to get ready. Most importantly I needed to lose weight. I was about 175 pounds at the time and decided I had my best chance of fighting around 150. Surely those little guys couldn't hurt me and I had gotten pretty proficient on the speed bag. I was working at a neighborhood liquor store, Sprits of America, and usually was the only one working during my shift. I usually ate there anyway since I didn't have much extra money in college, but now I decided the best way to eat but still lose weight was to simply not swallow. I could eat anything I wanted, chew it to enjoy the flavor, but then spit it into a brown paper bag and not add the calories. Genius.

I was well on my way to my 150-pound goal and decided it was time to get into a ring and spar with someone. Ernie was one of my fraternity brothers and also in the boxing club. He was a little smaller than me, probably a natural 150 pounder, and he was a nice guy. Maybe because growing up he was always on the smaller size and got picked on, or maybe because he was a wrestler all through high school, who knows, but fighting seemed to come easy to him. Regardless, I thought I should be able to hold my own pretty well with Ernie and it would be a good test. So, we decided to spar a few rounds.

I had an overhand right cross that was pretty effective and for the first few moments, it easily found its target which was Ernie's head. I think it caught Ernie off-guard at first but out of nowhere, he threw a straight right jab right square in my nose.

That was it. Memories of my experience with Kenny a decade earlier came flooding back. My nose hurt and I quit right then. Reality was laughing hard at me and taunting "take your dress and go home sissy boy". I did.

I don't often remember that experience with Ernie, but I do periodically hear my dad instructing me to implement the "Windmill". It's probably good advice in some situations. Going all in and giving it everything you have certainly is admirable. But just prepared for a punch in the nose, they can come from anywhere.

## <u>Chapter 38</u>

### Independence Day- Tim

When we are growing up and before we are teenagers, we are dependent on our parents for almost everything; food, shelter, clothes, transportation, etc. When we become teenagers, we started to want to break away from that dependency and at times even start to be embarrassed by our parents dropping us off at the movies, get-togethers with others, well just about anything where we needed a car to get there.

As we hit high school at age 15 or so we start to get a glimpse at the future and our semi-independence when we signed up for Driver's Education. We had to make sure to get the class completed before we turned 15 and 1/2 as that was the legal age to take the drivers written test at the DMV (Department of Motor Vehicles). This would let you drive a car (with a licensed driver in the passenger seat) to practice for the practical (driving) test. There were some restrictions like no driving on the freeway or driving at night. What I found out in the driver's education class was that you could also take the motorcycle written test and once passed, could obtain a driver's permit for a motorcycle. Again, some restrictions, no driving at night, no driving on the freeway, or no passengers on the back of the motorcycle.

My older brother and I wanted to start making our own money. We played sports after school, so we couldn't get an after-school job, but we could work in the summer. We received our work permits from school and away we went to get a summer job. My brother was able to get a job at a ranch that grew peaches and pears. You needed to be a minimum of 16 years of age to work there. He had just turned 16 in July as he was born in 1958. I was only 14 at that time (as we are 16 months apart). But I was successfully able to change my 1959 (birth year) on my work permit to show 1957. I was now 16 and I was able to get hired there also. We both got jobs driving tractors that pulled a trailer full of fruit bins (about 5 or 6 each). We would drive those tractor/trailers through the orchard rows and the people picking the fruit would dump it into the bins. Once they were full, we would drive them to the slab where we would get the bins taken off our trailers and new empty ones would be loaded onto them and we would do this routine many times a day ... all summer. Well, we were making $1.85/hr., which didn't seem like much, but it was enough for us to save a little money. We did this for many summers, but during the second summer when I was already 15 and 1/2, I had passed my DMV written motorcycle test and now had my motorcycle permit. It just happened that a neighbor across the street was selling (which I thought was the coolest motorcycle ever) a Honda XL 250 Enduro. I can't remember how much I paid (and my Dad may have even helped a little) but it must not have been more than $200.

This opened an entirely new world for me.  I remember heading out down every back road until I ended up way out in Camp Far West on top of a hill, looking out at the sun, straddling my motorcycle, and feeling like the King of the World.  I no longer needed my parents to drive me anywhere.  At 15 and 1/2 I had found my independence ... well at least my transportation independence :)

## Chapter 39

### Blessed Beyond Belief - Terry

I have been blessed to be given the life I have. I am so grateful that I had such loving parents and such amazing brothers.

I am always so proud to tell people about my wonderful family with the six boys and sister Cathy. Although we did not get the chance to meet her in this life, I know mom and dad are with Cathy in heaven.

I can always rely on the fact that when I meet up with my brothers, they are always going to be kind and happy to see me just as I am to see them. I am so proud of the honorable men that we all have become due to our upbringing. We can pass these traits on to our children, nieces, and nephews, and continue the legacy of being good productive Christian citizens of our communities.

With being blessed as we have, I feel that we should continue to show grace and love to one another even those who do you wrong. Thank you, God, for showing me the way and continue to bless all of us.

## Chapter 40

### The Call – Pat

How does one know they are being called by God? I have pondered this question for so many years and have even asked a variety of clergy. The responses have been as varied as those whom I have asked. There was one thing in common however, not one person had a "Paul on the road to Damascus" experience where a bright light and Christ's voice knocked them off a horse. Mostly it was an unfolding journey.

As for me, I am quite certain that God has called me not for anything special that I possess, but just the opposite. It is in my weakness, my inabilities, and my self-imposed crosses that He calls me to be better than I am.

My story is long, probably boring, and full of failures with a now and then small success. I would easily say I was a very self-centered boy and man. I always had a caring heart but

I think I cared more about my wants and needs than others. Even as a boy and young man I was quite gluttonous.

By the grace of God, He led a wonderful woman into my life with an inspiring spirit. After marriage, we moved to San Diego, CA, and after a few years, I was successful in opening a few very profitable businesses. There I was, after some time, just over thirty years of age and with a beautiful wife, three healthy children, a handful of thriving healthcare businesses, a large home on a hill overlooking the city, a boat we used to tour the waters around Mexico and the islands, a housekeeper, gardeners, and all the world could offer. At the same time, the world was showering us with its gifts, we were also engaging in our faith more and more. This must have been God trying to teach us or at least trying to open our eyes.

I am not sure how it happened or exactly when, but one day an idea formed in my mind so clearly and with such certainty. We had reached the "American Dream" that so many strive for, but I also had a deep emptiness. What happens when you strive for what you have always had been told would be the ultimate reward, the goal of life, to be financially well off, happily married, and blessed with children, but then you realize it isn't all that it was promised to be? Reaching the goal did not bring overwhelming peace and joy. It brought some confusion and anxiety. What were we to do now? Reaching the goal was to be the endmark on the journey. I think I must have had it all wrong. I began to pray for clarity. Then God zapped me with "Peace does not come from acquiring but from giving. Joy does not come by being served, but by serving others. Happiness cannot be earned but is freely given and received." This revelation which I knew was "Truth" rocked my world.

Our life journey then took a remarkable change in the path after that insightful revelation. We closed down our businesses and gave away most of our possessions. We moved to the very north of the state to Redding, California and started over. We rented a small house, and I took a job serving the HIV patients in the region. I would travel across northern California and visit those in their homes suffering from the deadly disease and tried to help them while they deteriorated. I learned much from those with their death sentence and how they looked at and lived their remaining life. I also began to study the faith more fervently and volunteered more through the Church. I began to see God and Christ more clearly in those around me, and I was also able to see his reflection in myself from time to time. I could sense God speaking to me in the quiet of my heart, and I listened. He eventually led me to the diaconate and after many years and through His grace the Church ordained me. After ordination, something changed within me. I am not able to describe the change in words, it is supernatural and hard to comprehend even for me. It is, however, extremely humbling and can be painful at times knowing what is expected and seeing my faults so clearly. Yet, I also see and feel His grace.

I remain probably just as imperfect as ever, still struggle with my crosses, and can be self-centered, prideful, and even lazy. Yet, I know God and can recognize Him in so many around me, in the opportunities He places in my life, and how He continues to call me to be better than I am. As a sinful person, broken in many ways, and a lowly man, I thank God for calling me towards Him and I will continue to strive to be His faithful, loving, and humble servant.

## <u>Chapter 41</u>

### Growing Old: The Next Chapter - Dan

Some people dread growing old. Knowing that their days are creeping away. I'm one of those that enjoy getting older. I will be turning 50 this year. I'm excited about that. Excited to make it another decade.

My perspective on life changes as the days go by. I am more at peace with what I've accomplished. I don't have the so-called "bucket list" that many people have. I am satisfied with the many experiences that I've had and don't feel like I've missed out or come up short.

I hope to live for a while longer. I enjoy life. I enjoy the outdoors and being active. Barbara and I can't wait to go live in another part of the country. Experience life in a different setting.

Our kids are raised now. We feel like there is no better time to venture out.

It is nice to sit back and watch our kids, grandkids, nieces, and nephews navigate their way through life. Watching them discover what their interests are. What gets their wheels turning. It's fun to see the joy of life in these younger kids, hearing their perspective on current events. Their ideas and beliefs don't always align with mine, but it's interesting none the less. I am excited to watch them grow and learn what their passions are, see their successes. It's really all about family.

This next chapter of my life is going to be great. Newly married. A partner that wants to explore the outdoors with me. Living in a new place, a new state. Just the two of us alone, by ourselves for the first time. I'm looking forward to growing older together

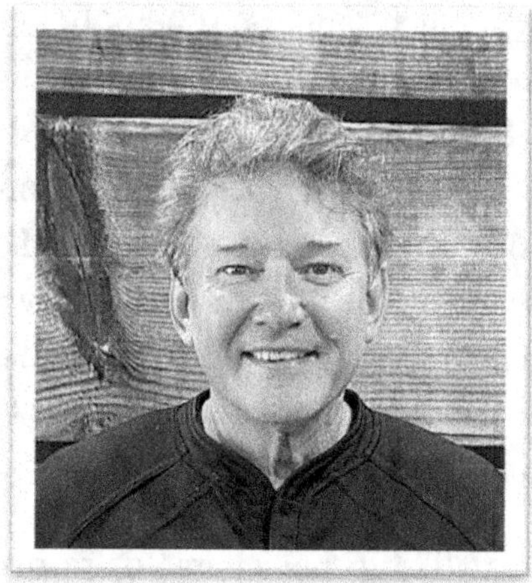

## Chapter 42

### One More Day-Kevin

My Dad has been gone now for over two decades. There may be a day now and then that passes that I do not think about him, but those are rare. When he was with us, he likely didn't realize just how much he impacted our lives. He did for sure, but thinking about it, his impact may have been even greater in the years since he passed.

A while back I found letters my mom wrote about me. I was the firstborn of six so Mom still had the energy to do this sort of thing. She wrote a letter every year on my birthday. At least for the first several years. It was more of a journal since it wasn't to anyone in particular. I went through a phase when I was not very loving towards my parents. I wasn't overtly mean and was probably a typical youngster thinking my parents knew nothing and certainly weren't cool. But being the first child, this was all new to my Dad and I think I may have broken his heart more than once. When I read those letters, I cried. How could I have caused my dad such sadness. If he only knew how much I would grow to admire him. How much I would realize I love him. How much I wish he were still here so I could show him. Everyday. When I was stupid young, I ran from him. Today I would use all my strength to run to him. I have so many questions for him. Some of these questions I was conscious of when he was still here. Some I never considered until later in life. Why didn't I ask them when I had the chance? I just need one more day with him.

What was it like to be separated from your siblings at such a young age? How did he deal with the embarrassment of psoriasis that covered so much of his body that he needed to apply salve and wrap himself in plastic wrap from head to toe at night? What was it like dealing with public perception when he decided to date one of his students? He was very honorable, and the relationship was based on love since he eventually married our mom, staying true to her for over 40 years of marriage until the day he died. But that had to be hard, especially in those days. What were his life regrets? Did his boys make him proud? Did I make Him proud? How. Why. What did he fear? Just being able to run my life choices past him now would be so comforting. I know I could trust he held no ulterior motives in his counsel. Why did it take me growing old to understand how valuable old wisdom can be? I really just need one more day with him.

How far would I go to get one more day? What would I give up? I probably wouldn't give up my eyesight. And the impact music has on my soul, more than likely would prefer not to give up my hearing. But what about my ability to speak? Maybe. I could still communicate by writing. So, yeah, maybe I would give up my ability to speak for something important. I would give it up if it gave my brother Mike his leg back. And his health. I would give it up for a chance to spend a day with my dad. I would hope it was worth a week but I would take a day. I would give up a finger. It would have to be the right finger though. I want to be able to signal certain things. Like its "ok". And what you can do to yourself if you are a bit of a turd. But I do have another hand so maybe it doesn't matter. I would give a finger if I could help my brother Terry avoid the fear of losing his career late in life. Or my brother Dan facing a fire that wiped out his house. Or my brother Pat for things that I'm sure scared him but I don't know because he is private. Or help Tim avoid that scary walk to his Kitty Hawk assignment. And even two fingers if Mike could avoid diabetes. Then again, they are all stronger and better for those experiences so maybe I will keep my digits. Unless it made me a better bowler. I have seen Dan and Tim get scary good with the two-finger roll.

I can imagine growing old with dad. When I was less than half the legal drinking age, I do recall finding my Dad's secret stash of Gin and Tom Collins mix. It was high above the stove in a cupboard. And actually, he rarely touched it. He rarely drank at all but now and then he would have a Tom Collins. If he had two, it was obvious. Not in a bad way, he was just animated. It never dawned on me that he might have chosen that drink because his name was Tom. Then again, probably not, he just was never that focused on himself. I would sure love to belly up to a bar and share one with him now.

One example that will forever burn bright in my heart is how much he loved his wife, our mom. No matter how challenging she made life, and she definitely could create obstacles, he just never wavered in his love for her. Thankfully he didn't suffer from Alzheimer's, he passed too quickly and too young. But I could imagine him losing his memory and even then when all else seemed forgotten, just mentioning mom and surely his eyes would light up. How he loved her. And us. God, I miss him. I wish I would have known how much I would miss him when I still had him. I just need one more day to let him know.

But then, that one day would only reveal even more just how special my dad was. Still is. Having that insight, I would gain from my one extra day with him I fear I would miss him even more than I do now. It would hurt too much. So, I will just have to be satisfied with what I have now, a thankfulness for having him as my dad. Unanswered questions and all.

My dad wasn't perfect. But he was better than me. And if I just patterned my life after his, imperfect as he was, I would be a better me. What would Jesus do? Come on, He was God. But what would Dad do? Now that's a human I could shoot for.

Darn it Dad, you left too soon. I just need one more day.

## Chapter 43

## Adventures On The High Seas - Tim

I was stationed onboard the USS Kitty Hawk CV-63. (Carrier Vessel – Aircraft Carrier). I lived on board that ship from 1983-1986. We went on many battle group training exercises and two 7-month Westpac (western pacific) deployments. Here are some of the adventures I participated in during that time.

Since we are trapped in this floating building when out at sea, all the sailors became firefighters. Many of us (who lead make-shift firefighting teams while on-board) attended firefighting school. We wore all the heavy fire resistance clothes and OBA (Oxygen Breathing Apparatus) masks while carrying large water hoses. The instructors would lead us into buildings where they had set many different types of fires that we may encounter on the ship. Fire and smoke were everywhere and we would have to enter the room and sweep the base of the fire (depending on which type) and put the fire out before we could back out to safety. Luckily, we never had any fires on the ship during any of our deployments. The aircraft carrier had many helicopters, F-14 jets, and many other aircraft on it either down in the hangar bay or up on the flight deck. There were two catapults on the flight deck up in the front third of the ship. There were 3 or 4 catch wires or landing cables toward the rear half of the ship. The catapults would hook to the front of the jets and pull them along the flight deck (the jets were in full throttle also) and launch them off the bow like a slingshot. The jets would land (touch down) with a hook connected to the rear of the plane that would drag on the flight deck and hook the cable which would slow the jet down and it would extend until the plane stopped. When a plane would grab this cable and stretch it there would be a VERY loud dragging and unwinding sound it would make. Then the cable would retract winding itself back up with the equally LOUD dragging sound until back in place. I lived in a barracks just under the flight deck and my rack was directly under the 2nd cable (which seemed to be the one most planes would grab). Night after night, the flight ops would continue, and the jet would land right over my head with a crashing thump and then the cable dragging scenario would continue. The funny thing is that after a few nights, I could sleep right through that entire routine and still hear my little watch alarm softly beep to wake me up to go to work. The mind is a master of adaptation. I also remember my buddy and me, after flight ops would end for the night, climbing out onto the platforms that hung over the front of the bow with nothing but water below us and laying on our backs, looking up at the stars, thousands of miles from any land and just shooting the breeze. We felt like we were on a cloud as the bow of the ship would rise and fall about 50 feet over and over again while navigating along the ocean waves.

During these deployments, we would stop off at many countries to refuel (we did this at sea sometimes by getting fuel lines shot across from a fueling ship to ours and we would have to drag these massive fuel hoses into place all while trying to not have the ships crash into each other. Anyway, we would stop in many countries for fuel, repairs, restock our food supplies, etc. We stopped in Hawaii, the Philippines, Sri Lanka, Australia, etc. When we would pull into these ports, half the crew would get to go on liberty (leave from the ship) for half the time we were there and then the other half of the crew would get to leave on the 2nd half of our stay. I remember we arrived in Columbo, Sri Lanka. Our ship was so large that we had to anchor out quite away from shore and smaller boats would come and pick us up and take us to shore. We had been out at sea this time for 70 straight days without seeing land. I was lucky enough to be in the first half of the crew to get to leave the ship first. We were going to be in Sri Lanka for 4 days and we would get to explore the island for the first two. The seas were very rough that first day and we had to lower the hanger bay elevators (this carried the planes between the hanger bay and the flight deck. We lowered the hanger bay elevators as low as we could and us sailors would time when the boats below would be close enough to jump into when they got near the elevator. The seas were so rough that the boats kept coming close and then would get pushed away, back and forth this continued. Well, we all got carried over to the island and had a great time for the first two days. Then the weather got worse the last two days and the boats couldn't carry the second half of the crew to the island, so we got to stay on the island all 4 days. It was fantastic (for us that made it on the island).  Well, when the 4 days were up, the seas were still just as bad, so they needed to send helicopters from the ship to the island to bring us back.  That was exciting and the crew members that didn't get to visit the island were not too happy with us (and probably didn't talk to us or want to hear our stories for a few days).  They were the first off, the ship on our next port – the Philippines, but it wasn't that big of a deal as we had been there seven times already.

I would tell you about the initiation we had to go through as we crossed the international dateline on our way to Australia to become "trusty shellbacks," but I might be stripped of my membership if I do so.

Let me leave you with one more adventure, as I could probably write a book of these adventures all by themselves. One of the most exciting tasks I had was to accompany the Chaplain from our ship (which was so large that it didn't move on the water like smaller ships) so he could perform church services for the sailors on those ships that didn't have Chaplains.  Our ship would rise and fall gradually, so you never felt seasick like on smaller ships in our surrounding battle group.  Well, we couldn't pull over in the middle of the ocean to walk from one ship to the other, so how did we get there?  He and I would get in a helicopter and take off from the flight deck of the carrier.  We would fly over and hover over one of the other ships the Chaplain was going to perform services on.  The thing is the ships never stopped.  They never even slowed down.  We would be hovering over the littler ship, flying sideways, and staying at the same speed as the other ships.  We would then be connected to cables and lowered down out of the helicopter onto the deck of the smaller ship.  Because we were on the water and the electricity generated by the propellers of the helicopter, a crewmember on the deck of the smaller ship, would hook the cable we were being lowered on with that metal hook that was grounded on the deck of their ship.  This would have to happen before our feet making contact with the ship to keep us from getting electrocuted.  Once on board, I would help set up the service and then hang out with the crew until the Chaplain was finished.  Then we would go to another ship in this manner.  I do remember while waiting on the smaller ships getting a little seasick as they would rock and roll.  I would finally be glad to get back to our floating city to settle my stomach. These are some of the adventures aboard the USS Kitty Hawk.

## Chapter 44

### Rise And Shine - Terry

Every morning I wake up and thank God for the day He has blessed us with and thank Him for all the wonderful opportunities that lie ahead. I pray to God that the people that I encounter on this day will see God's light shine through me as I greet them with a kind smile.

Each day I take a few moments to think about all the blessings I have been given and I am so thankful for the path I am on. I come from a loving caring family. I have awesome children and a wonderful and awesome and beautiful Christian wife. I am an optimistic person that sees the glass half-full and I rise and shine with the idea that each day is going to be great. I never really know how the day is going to go, but I try to be the best person I can be for that day. Our time on earth is just a blink of the eye in terms of eternity so do not get down and depressed over things that you cannot control. Wake up each day with the idea that spending eternity with God is all that matters and try to serve others and you will notice your life will seem much better. God bless you all.

## Chapter 45

## My Reflection

Maybe it takes numerous years and an abundance of successes and failures to begin to see who we are with a clear lens. I am now able to see a few gifts that God has bestowed upon me, but I am more clearly able to see my faults and inabilities. I wish I were more disciplined. I wish I had greater virtue. I wish I had greater devotion. I wish, I wish, and I wish.

My only consolation is in that of Jesus who stated in the great Beatitudes that **Blessed are the Poor in Spirit**. In my theology training I learned that this meant that those who wanted to be closer to God, realized that they were still far from having an intimate relationship with Him, were those who were actually Poor in Spirit. It was in that recognized poverty and in their desire that they were blessed because they had the insight into knowing what they were lacking, and that they wanted more.

I know what I am lacking, that is clear, and I do want more. I feel that God has called me to be something greater than

I currently am, and it is only me that keeps getting in the way of my true calling (Who God created me to be). Yes, I am Poor in Spirit. But where do I turn?

Year after year my desire to be better doesn't change, yet do I change?

I was once told that the closer we grow towards Christ the more our darkness is revealed. Meaning, that in our reflection of such holiness our reflection reveals a stark contrast between us and Christ. And when you place side-by-side our being against the One who is truth, beauty, and reality, we pale to compare.

I believe it is Saint John of the Cross who shared such great insight into the Dark Night of the Soul and the Dark Night of the Spirit.

Yet, this peeling back of our deep darkness, our self-centeredness, our pride, our envy, our greed, doesn't have to be an obstacle or a point of despair, it can be a starting point of truthfulness and an opportunity to deepen our faith and relationship with God. In the acceptance of our failures and with the spirit to change our ways, to grow in holiness, to separate ourselves from the ways of the world, we can become free.

Thanks be to God for his graciousness to show us our weaknesses and to allow us to change our ways before it is too late to change.

## Chapter 46

## My Life So Far - Dan

Life is definitely a journey. It can include the highest of highs and the lowest of lows. Some people may work harder than others in capturing their success, others may stumble across it by chance. Then you have those people whose lives are littered with one disappointment after another, no matter how strong their efforts are.

I often ponder my life and where it falls in comparison to others. Did I meet or exceed my expectations? Did I fall short? What or whose standards am I trying to reach? How do you measure success?

Looking back at my adolescent years, I fondly remember the many adventures I had. Playing games with friends, riding bicycles to wherever we wanted to go. Shooting BB guns, fishing, swimming, you name it. We were always outside living it up. My childhood friends and I have all drifted apart in proximity to one another, but our memories we share forever. I was a happy kid, so I consider that part of my life as a success. Moving into young adulthood is when life became a little scarier. Finishing high school, completing college, and ultimately starting a career and family. No longer were Mom and Dad there to shelter and care for me. It was time to make a name for myself.

I married a woman who had an 11-year-old daughter and an 8-year-old son, and we had one on the way. I instantly became a family man. At about the same time, I started a brief career in retail management, but quickly realized the long hours, minimal pay and grouchy customers weren't for me. Before long I discovered a career in the financial services world and for a time, found my calling. I would work in this world for the next 17 years. Made plenty of money at times and not so much at other times. That career and my marriage would ultimately end, about the time our youngest daughter graduated high school. Mixed results during these years to say the least. However, raising 3 kids who are doing great today, I consider this part of my life a success.

Fast forward to today. I have a new career going on 7 years now, and it is going okay. It won't be my final job. I still believe that a fulfilling position is out there somewhere. But I'm okay if I don't find it. What I care about, is this wonderful woman that I will be marrying a week from now. We attended the same schools from elementary through high school. Acquaintances during those years, but nothing else. Nearly 30 years later, after each of us going through the trials and tribulations of life, we found each other. She is the most incredible person I know. We enjoy each other so much. She is my best friend. I feel pretty successful right now.

I'm not sure what the next years hold for me. I do know that God has been there for me every step of this journey. I also know that I am going to try to enjoy every minute of it. I am so thankful for all of the amazing people that I've met and the relationships that have formed along the way.

## Chapter 47

## My Bucket List - Kevin

My life has been blessed in so many ways. That's not to say I haven't had my share of challenges, but the "good" has outweighed the "bad" to such a great degree. I know without a doubt there are at least a billion people that would trade me places on even my most trying day and would think they won the lottery. I am thankful every day for the path God has me walking.

I have been very fortunate; my life has been filled with so many cool experiences:
- Learning to fly a plane,
- Skydive,
- Scuba dive,
- Paraglide,

- Travel the world and visiting over 40 countries in my work,
- Having multiple dogs and horses.
- Surviving stage 4 cancer,
- Surviving diverticulosis in a third world country,

OK, these last two are not really on anyone's bucket list, but just sharing to show what a varied and full life I have enjoyed. The list goes on and on. As a result, I am often asked what is left on my bucket list. When I think about it, I never have had a bucket list. I didn't grow up with a passion for adventure or a desire to travel. I don't think I even have adrenaline; I doze in the plane just before we jump for gosh sakes. Things have just sort of worked out that way.

I am far from a completed, fully evolved project though. I laugh at the mere thought that the journey is nearing completion, in all honesty, it has only just started. If I did have a bucket list, it wouldn't be filled with experiences, and certainly not a desire for material possessions…. No, it would be focused more on ways I could improve as a person. In my mind, I can picture a version of me that I wish I could be. I wish I was more patient. I wish I could think before I speak and then be more sensitive with my words. No doubt I care about people, I do.

I have no hesitation sharing the many blessings God has bestowed on me. But often that kind of sharing, monetary or material possessions, are easy. Much more challenging would be to consistently kindly listen and then reflecting carefully and thoughtfully before responding. A huge improvement would be evolving such that I could put myself in another's shoes and try imaging their perspective, especially when it conflicts with mine.

I don't want to realize one day I have become that "Get off my lawn" old guy. I will always be thankful for what I have and even more for what I can share. But my bucket list is short, a simple pursuit to be a kinder, gentler version, more open to differing perspectives. And counting to ten before I speak.

## Chapter 48

### A Simple Thing Like A Beer - Tim

This story is a brief description of an adventure my brother Pat and I went on.  We may someday write a book in more detail of the numerous encounters and sites each day along the trail and our final descent into Santiago de Compostela, but for now, here we go –

My brother Pat and I went on an amazing and life-changing adventure in France and Spain in 2017.  We hiked a big part of the Camino de Santiago – the Way of Saint James trail.  We went in August when it is usually hot there, so we trained in over 100-degree temperatures here in the United States with heavy packs on our backs.  Although it was tough, it paid off as we did exceptionally well during the actual hike there.

Our first two days were tough as there were huge inclines as we climbed and crossed over the French Pyrenees Mountains into northern Spain.  We only allotted two weeks to traverse this trail although it takes a month to walk it, we decided to split up the walk into two parts.  The climb out of France into Spain hiking the first quarter of the Saint James Way trail and then take a train over to a city 118 kilometers out from Santiago de Compostela and hike the last quarter of the trail.  We ended up hiking approximately 300 kilometers of the 500 kilometers hike (we got a few more kilometers in as we ventured off in the evenings to explore different places in the villages we would stay in, like a fountain that dispensed water from one spigot and wine from another).  Yes, we got wine from one of them.

We were able to see the most exciting parts of the hike doing it this way.  After a couple of days, the daily hikes seemed to get easier.  The best terrain for us was rolling hills as it put pressure on different parts of our feet and legs and we could walk farther and farther.  We even hiked 25 miles one day (40k).

This hike was amazing.  People do this hike for many reasons, but our focus was on the spiritual.  We were not disappointed.  It seemed like God was showing us special places that others on the walk were missing.  For example, we would be hiking for hours with many other hikers spread out along the trail.  Out of nowhere and walking in the opposite direction a woman stopped us on the path and told us if we walked up this steep hill, we would see a beautiful old church that we wouldn't want to miss.  We were the only ones to veer off the path and climbed up to see the most mesmerizing very old church.  When we went inside, two caretaker ladies asked us to follow them up to a room on the second floor (closed off to the public) and there were statues of many of the saints so beautifully carved.  We were in awe of such beauty and without the unexpected happening of the little old lady that seemed to come out of nowhere and let us in on this secret, we would never have been able to bask in such glory.

What also made this trip in Spain so enjoyable was that Pat and I could speak Spanish.  Pat could speak much better than I could, but we were able to communicate with the Spanish residents.  I'm sure this helped with the church caretakers as they spoke no English.  In the larger towns we walked through, some of the locals spoke English, but it was rare in the smaller villages we hike through.  We even had a full-on conversation with a farmer tending to his cow in his barn as we passed by.  We spoke with him for about 30 minutes and we were able to make each other laugh … speaking only in Spanish.

After hiking many miles each day (starting before the sun came up with our headlamps on) we would finish around 3 pm and quickly wash our clothes in a sink, hang them out to dry, and take a quick shower at our 5 Euro a night accommodation.  We would then walk to the nearest café and order an Estrella Galicia beer and reminisce on the adventures we partook in that day.  That beer was like drinking liquid from heaven.  We would look forward to this beer each day before we finally ate dinner and went to sleep with backpacks ready at the foot of our bunks for the early morning departure.

## Chapter 49

**The Secret To Happiness - Terry**

I have learned through many years that if you help others and be generous you will find happiness and fulfillment in your life. Most people find when they are feeling sad or depressed, they are thinking about themselves. All thoughts of being mistreated, ignored, not respected, or not loved can be erased from your mind when you stop thinking about yourself and start focusing on helping others. By making your life less about you and committing yourself to be a good servant of God you will find an inner peace that will take over and a light will shine through you instead of you being the person that needs to be rescued.

Any time I start feeling defeated, sad, or depressed, I try to remember to be grateful for all the positive things in my life and then move on to helping others. The point is the less you think in selfish terms the happier you will be. Remember most hard times are short and you can get through anything with God's help. Life is a series of habits, good or bad, so try to develop good habits, pray daily, and you will enjoy a very fruitful life.

## Chapter 50

### Escape From Idaho – Pat

Liz and I had always dreamed of living outside of California. After our missionary year in Guatemala, we had the perfect opportunity. We had very few possessions and had already sold our house the year before. We contemplated various states: Texas, New Mexico, Arizona, and even the East Coast. We ultimately settled on the state of Idaho. We had heard that it was a conservative state and was not too far away from California and that was a benefit for visiting family. I was able to secure a job in Western Idaho at a large medical center doing psychiatric nursing which was my field of work.

The people of Idaho seemed nice and the pace was much slower than California, but not as slow as Guatemala. I received an assignment to Our Lady of the Valley Parish in Caldwell, and we fell in love with the pastor, the parishioners, and the entire community. The people were hungry for the faith, and although many of the parishioners knew their faith quite well, probably due to Father Flores and his Orthodox teachings, yet, the parishioners still wanted more. I started a men's group where men could go camping together and receive a spiritual retreat at the same time. That concept resonated well with the Idahoans who love the outdoors. I also started a podcast with six Catholic friends called the Idaho Catholic Podcast, and we would meet weekly to have pizza and beer and then record a session on various topics related to living the Catholic faith in the modern world. The popularity of the podcast grew, and in no time we had hundreds of loyal listeners.

All things seemed to be going well in Idaho, but after a few years, something seemed to be missing. It was family. I still had five brothers in California, and Liz had her father there. Her mother was living in Montana. We missed our immediate family. Sure, we loved our church family, and I had some of the best friends I had ever had in my life. But God was somehow telling me that I (we) needed to go home.

Doing what we do and trusting the urges of the Spirit we quickly made up our minds and decided we were leaving. We were going to be one of the few families returning to California when so many were escaping California. Yet, we felt determined. I accepted a job as a Chief Nursing Officer at a large psychiatric hospital in Sacramento, and in just a few weeks we were back in California and reunited with our families.

Liz's mom must have decided that she was being called back to California, too, since it wasn't long, and she left Montana and moved in with us.

Now back in California, I was assigned to Saint Joseph Parish in Marysville, my childhood parish. Many of my brothers are joining me at Mass each week, and we are building a close and intimate relationship centered on the love we have for each other and the love inspired by our shared faith. I have this very special feeling that God called me (us) back home for a special purpose that He will reveal when the time is right, and possibly that it has to do with my brothers and our faith. I am so excited to see where He leads and takes us on this wonderful life journey.

## <u>Chapter 51</u>

**Favorite Memories With My Brothers - Dan**

I have lived a blessed life. It is a life that has been made better by having 5 brothers to share it with. They have made such a huge impact on who I am today. I believe that I am a glass-half-full kind of guy. I can attribute a lot of that to my mom and dad and how they raised us. Always look forward and not back. Make the right decisions and you will be so much better off. When you make mistakes, truly learn from it and grow.

As the years have gone by, and with our parents in heaven, I have leaned on my brothers for love and support. Every one of them has that positive, can-do attitude. It can't help but rub off on me. I wanted to take this opportunity to acknowledge the best memory I have with each of them. There are so many to list, but I will keep it to one.

My brother Mike. So close in age. I could list a million memories. I would say the time he was in the service. He was living at Camp Pendleton in Southern California. He invited me to come to see him. I'm guessing I was maybe 19. We spent the weekend going to a comedy club, a baseball game, the ocean, and so on. It was one of the first times that we had hung out together since school and living as young adults now. It reconfirmed that we would always be best friends despite where life took us.

As I go down the line, the age difference between myself and my brothers' increases. The memories are of us as adults, at various stages of our lives.

My brother Pat. I would have to say the memory that stands out the most is when my Mother was in her last few days of life. My Mom was living with me and was on hospice. Pat would come over daily to check in on all of us. The spiritual comfort that he provided for Mom and me is something I'll never forget. Pat has a way and still does of making everyone feel that it will be okay.

My brother Terry. I have many memories from camping to triathlons to kayaking. Narrowing it down to one, I would say it was when Terry brought his new girlfriend to watch my baseball game during my senior year. I thought it was so cool, as I think this was their first date. Who knew his friend Debi would turn into being his wife, now going on 30 years.

My brother Tim. Again, so many memories. Always down to do anything. Especially any sport or activity. All of the brothers were on sports teams growing up, but I'm not sure if any of us were on the same team very often. Tim and I were living in Redding at the time. We would go to a club and play tennis often. We heard that they had a tennis team, and we decided that we would join it. As a doubles team. We never played doubles and never as a team. We gelled instantly. Our success was amazing. We never lost a match. Our team advanced through sections and went to regionals in Carmel. Although our club team failed to advance further, it was not because of us. We destroyed the competition every time. Each of us had experienced success individually and with others, but never as teammates. Pretty cool.

My brother Kevin. The furthest apart in age at 13 years. That hasn't prevented us from growing so close as the years have gone by. My best memory was when Kevin put together a trip of a lifetime. He took me to Dallas to attend a Cowboys game. Not just any game. It was Sunday night football with my childhood hero, Roger Staubach. I'm talking about going to Roger's house and looking at all of his awards. Holding his Heisman trophy. Man, that was heavy. Riding over in the same vehicle as Roger, and parking where all the players do. Entering the stadium from underneath to Roger's suite. Watching the game with all the food and drinks you wanted. What an unbelievable weekend.

I have to say I am very blessed. My brothers are all amazing people. Not just for all of the unforgettable experiences that they've given me, but for the type of guys that they are. Every one of them would do anything for anyone.

## **Chapter 52**

**Blessed By Cancer -Kevin**

I have always been relatively healthy. Growing up one of six brothers, we all certainly had our fair share of bumps and bruises. Even my experiences that should have turned out much worse, like falling off a three-story house in college or developing diverticulitis in a third-world country, still only resulted in a few broken bones and an extremely painful but successful hospital stay respectively. All in all, pretty tame. So, it usually comes as a surprise when I share that for some unknown reason, I just always knew one day I would have cancer. It wasn't a morbid prediction, nor did it consume me with fear. I rarely thought about it, it was just a distant feeling.

My fifty-first birthday had just been celebrated and I was cruising through life. Then, for some unknown reason, I reached deep in my throat and discovered a lump. No pain, no discomfort, no reason to be sticking my fingers that far back at all. I almost forgot about it until I was at a routine dentist appointment. Almost an afterthought, I asked my dentist to check it out. He thought it was quite unremarkable, but just to be safe, he recommended I go see an ENT Doc friend of his. But it was probably nothing. With no sense of urgency, I reached out to his friend and scheduled an appointment.

The ENT doc was a nice guy, and his quick assessment was that it was likely nothing to be concerned about, but let's take a biopsy just to be sure. He took a sample and said he would call me in a week. The next day while shopping at Costco, I was a bit surprised to get a call, and "caller ID" announced it was my ENT Doc. The call that was supposed to come in a week was now ringing after only one day. I answered and in my best bugs bunny tone asked, "What's up doc"? He greeted me and then followed with a very succinct, "you have cancer". No lead-up, no small talk, just very direct. But also very calm. I asked if it was the bad kind and he said "well, there isn't a good kind", but that he was sure we caught it very early and likely would only need a simple surgery to remove it. He said I needed to come in for a PET scan to make sure, but didn't seem worried, he was sure it was Stage 1 at worst.

I was able to go in for the scan right away and afterward, they said they would reach out to me with the results in a few days. I know it should probably have been more worrisome, but for some reason, I just wasn't alarmed. Well, until the call that was supposed to come in a few days came that very next morning. I asked what the results were and they said I needed to come in that day to see the Oncologist. I asked if they could give me a hint and they said best to just come in. When I got there, I met with the oncologist who asked me what I knew. I shared that my understanding was that although it was cancer, it was still in very early stages and could likely be removed with a simple surgery. He very calmly said no, that it was Stage 4 and that it had spread through the lymph nodes in my neck and I was not a candidate for surgery. I needed to start chemotherapy and radiation right away. But he also said that treatment had advanced tremendously in the last couple of years and my chances were much better. I wasn't sure how to interpret that so I asked what my prognosis was. He said with a huge smile, that he was optimistic and felt comfortable that my chance for recovery might even be as high as 50/50. I let that soak in for a moment then blurted out "50/50?! And that's an improvement?! What would they have been a year or two ago?". He said 90/10 and not in my favor. Now I could see why he was so happy….

I left his office and sat in my car. It dawned on me then that I probably should have brought someone with me to the appointment. At that moment I felt quite alone. I wasn't sure how to share this life-changing discovery with my family or loved ones. It all seemed a bit surreal, yet at the same time, not unexpected. Weird, I know. I knew I had a tough road ahead, but I also felt a strange comfort that it would all be ok. I had complete trust in God's plan for me, whatever that might be, so figured let's just get after it. Looking back, I also had no clue what was coming.

What I hadn't anticipated was the abundance of blessings that I would encounter along my path to recovery. Yes, I did fully recover. The journey wasn't easy, and in fact, was very touch and go for a while, but all the pain and misery paled in comparison to the love and support I was blessed with along the way. Family and friends who came to my rescue. Giving up vacation days, some traveling many miles, to share the load of driving me to treatment daily. Making sure I was getting the nutrients I desperately needed through my feeding tube because I lost the ability to swallow early on. Unselfishly cleaning me up after the multiple vomiting sessions I would enjoy each day. Making me go to daily treatment even when I was giving up. And praying for me. Constantly. I would mention my saviors by name but you know who you are. I know who you are. I will never forget you. Each one of you truly blessings. Maybe one day I will write a book chronicling my journey and then I can give each of you the credit you deserve.

People ask me if I had a different outlook on life after my experience. Honestly, not really. I was already blessed with an optimistic view of life before and my faith was strong. I did have a newfound realization that God had prepared me though. I was lucky to have been given parents who led by example when dealing with the many hardships they encountered. So many times when their struggles seemed at their darkest hour, I was amazed at how they found such strength in just "giving it to God and trusting". So many times when my fight seemed at its fiercest moments, I drew upon their example. My mom especially had consistently demonstrated such an amazing faith when confronted with her demons. She easily could have, should have, felt sorry for herself, and complained about how life was so unfair. Instead, she simply gave thanks for the challenges, claiming they were such a wonderful opportunity to show God her faith. Little did I know then how much strength I would derive from her example when I needed it most.

I also simply felt very blessed. Very blessed to have had cancer because it was only through that experience that I was able to realize just how deep and unwavering the love was from my family, loved ones, and friends. It would have been so easy for any of them to feign caring but hope that someone else stepped up to help. But none of them faltered. Everyone rising above and beyond to help me through to the finish line. Such blessings, each one of them.

I wouldn't wish cancer on anyone. Survival is not guaranteed, often not even likely, and the pain along the way is no fun. But it can also be a blessing in many ways. I know mine was. Thank God.

## Chapter 53

### Cowboy - Tim

I remember watching old westerns on TV with our Dad and idolizing the cowboys and dreaming of the life they lived. As we grew up in the suburbs, some of our school mates had horses, but we were never close enough to those schoolmates to get to ride those animals. I was always fascinated by these powerful and majestic beasts. As I got older, I was able to go on a couple of organized trail rides where you would get on the horse and stay in a line of many horses and just seemed to be along for the ride. I had no idea how to control or even steer the horse as it would just follow the one in front of him. Although still very fun, the horse was just a mystery to me. Well, as in so many adventures I have been blessed to have participated in, the catalyst is my brother Kevin. He was the one who got me to start snowboarding, skydiving, scuba diving, and now horse riding. We are taking riding lessons and staring to get more proficient at walking, trotting, and loping (cantering) the horses. The best part is that Kevin owns (4) horses and we have been riding (2) of them several times a week. Not only do we train on them, solo or with the trainer's guidance, but we do everything with them. We feed them, brush them, tack them up (put on their saddle, bridle, etc), clean out their hoofs, liberty work in the round pen, etc. We are starting to bond with them. When we let them loose in the arenas, they follow us around when we walk away from them. We are starting to feel like cowboys. Now, this is the fun part. The not so fun part is mucking out the stalls, unloading the hay bales from trucks with hay hooks, humping all the bed shavings and absorption pellets for their paddocks, etc. Since the horses are being boarded at a ranch we don't own, much of this "not so fun" stuff is handled by the ranch crew, but we have dreams of having our own ranch and barn in the future and then we will have to take care of this ourselves or hire our own crew.

From the time as a young child watching westerns with our Dad in front of the TV to now being able to partner with the horse just blows my mind. I feel blessed by the opportunities God (and my brother) have given me.

## Chapter 54

### Dedication To My Brothers – Terry

For my last story, I wanted to write about my brothers and what a privilege and honor it has been to be part of this family. All of my brothers are very talented and blessed with incredible gifts. I will list them in order from oldest to youngest and give a little description through my eyes.

Kevin is the oldest brother and has led the way for all of us to follow. He is very loving and caring for all the brothers and always checks in with everyone to make sure they are doing well. Kevin loves adventure and is always trying new things. He has done so many things in his life such as skydiving, scuba diving, owning a yacht, learning to fly a plane, and now he even owns horses. He is fearless in terms of trying new things and is always very impressive with his lease on life. Kevin will always be there for you if you need him.

Tim is the next brother I want to talk about. Tim is so smart, he has learned multiple languages, he taught himself how to play many musical instruments. He works in very competitive computer industry and he again is self-taught and one of the smartest people I know. Tim also is very loving and caring for others and is always there with an encouraging word. Tim also has a zest for adventure as he is a skydiver, scuba diver, hiker and he has competed in many triathlon events.

Pat is next in line and he is so exceptional as well. Pat is an ordained Deacon in the Catholic Church and has dedicated his life to serving the Lord. He is also a chief nursing officer in a mental hospital. I am always amazed at how Pat can get up in front of so many people at church and give a heartfelt homily without missing a beat. Pat also has a podcast that he is sharing God's powerful message with personal insights in a way that only Pat can deliver. Pat is a loving and caring family man to his wife and children and is a tremendous role model for all of us. He has written many Christian books and with his duties at the church, I am always in awe of how he can accomplish so much in one day.

Mike is my next brother that I would like to talk a little about. Mike has a heart of gold and all he wants to do is to please the people around him with his comedy or with any helping hand he can give. Mike loves everyone and I can tell by his Facebook page that he has so many friends and unlike a lot of other people, Mike has built solid relationships with all these people. Mike has had many health challenges over the years but he is so tough and he still is concerned with the welfare of others over himself. Mike shares his heart and soul with everyone and is loved by so many in return. Mike has a very loving and supporting wife and children who see what a terrific man he is.

Dan is my youngest brother but equally as impressive as all the others. Dan is the most positive person I have ever met and his personality is infectious. Dan is a star athlete who is so gifted when it comes to athletic skills. Dan has maintained so many friendships that he has made over the decades. He loves everyone he meets and they all love to hang around him in return. I would say that Dan is a people person. Dan is a dedicated family man and it shows. Dan has had to endure many hardships in life but he finds a way to overcome them with his attitude, and he ends up victorious and stronger than he was before.

Even though these little descriptions of my brothers do not even come close to telling the full story of their incredible lives, I am so proud to call them my brothers. All my brothers are good God-fearing people and very productive members of the communities in which they live. I love them all so much. God Bless them all.

## <u>Chapter 55</u>

### Friday Night Poker – Dan

I love it when I see a group of old men sitting down together. Usually in a doughnut shop or a restaurant. I often wonder what their story is. How long have they known each other? How many years have they been getting together regularly?

Though not in that age group yet, I like to think of my poker group in these terms. On the first Friday of every month, for the last 17 years, a group of about 8-10 guys get together to play poker. It's not about the money, as we only put in a few dollars. It's about getting together and laughing, mixed in with some good-natured smack talk.

A lot can happen when you've had a club for that long. During this time, we've had marriages, career changes, babies, and so on. You see each other's lives unfold before your eyes. In a way, you become a family. Everybody gets along and wants the best for each other.

The cool thing about our group is that we alternate who is responsible for the food. We've had BBQ's, chili, Mexican food, pizza, and so much more. We used to alternate which house we would play at. However, for the last several years we've played in a warehouse. One of the members owns a business there, so it feels like we've got our own underground poker game. I've always liked to compare it to the Sopranos, but my wife likes to refer to it as the He-Man Woman-Hater's Club. Kind of like the one they had on the Little Rascals.

I could tell story after story about the crazy things that have happened over the years. But what happens in the poker group, stays in the poker group. Great memories with great guys.

# Photo Gallery

**Kearns Family circa 1983**

**Betty Kearns and Boys**

**Mom and Dad plus Kevin, Tim, Terry**

**Thomas Walter Kearns (Teacher)**

**Tim USN**

**Mike USN**

**Brothers Podcasting 2019**

**Brothers 2019**

**Kevin and Tim 2020**

**Trail Riding Kevin and Tim 2020**

**Cowboys - Kevin and Tim 2020**

**Kevin and Tim**

**Brothers Circa 1988**

**Kevin, Tim, Terry, Pat**

**Tom and Betty Kearns**

**Mom, Dad, plus Kevin, Tim, and Terry**

**Betty Kearns in her twilight years**

**Tom Kearns with Grandchildren Jeneah and Sean**

**Pat Circa 1989**

**Thomas Kearns (Dad)**

**Brothers at Mass with Deacon Pat**

**The Brothers 2018**

**Annual Christmas Family Gathering**

**Pat and Tim (Camino de Santiago 2017)**

# Reflections
# on Creating
# the "Brothers" Book

## Kevin

If you had asked me several months ago if I thought the six of us would "want" to write a book of random stories about experiences we had growing up, I would have said "sure". If you then would have asked me if I thought we would pull it off, I would probably have said "not so sure". And if you would have asked me if I thought we would have produced over 50 stories; I probably would have been even less certain.

Shouldn't underestimate my brothers though. Probably silly to have expected there not to be an element of competition either. Seemed every time there was a lull in producing stories, someone would send one and the race to ten would be rekindled. My challenge was trying to figure out which stories to share. There were some memories that I thought would be appreciated, and those stories were easy. Some recollections though seemed too personal and I wondered if I should share those, or if anyone would even appreciate what they meant to me. I decided to take a chance on some. I was caught off guard at times when emotions would seem to come from out of the blue while transferring my thoughts into text, often experiencing emotional moments just "voicing" what I had never shared prior.

It didn't take long to realize that ten stories would only scratch the surface, there are so many more. Most of the stories in this book focus on earlier times growing up and where I have come from. And I think that was the intent of this edition, it was mine anyway. There are so many other aspects of my life which are important today, my partner Carol, dogs, horses, charities…. where I am and more importantly, where I am going. But those will have to wait for volume 2.

I was impressed with the quality and depth of feeling my brothers shared in their stories. Each has their own style of writing, so fitting for their personalities. Each brother caused me to discover something new about them and the unexpected benefit from this project is that I know them better and for which I am very thankful.

Some friends have commented they would never be able to get their siblings to collaborate on a similar book. I find that odd. Maybe I shouldn't though, maybe that is the norm. It's probably why I will cherish this experience with my brothers, it has been special.

## Tim

Writing a book with my brothers sounded like a fun project.  I thought coming up with 10 stories each was going to be a huge task though.  Many interesting and heartfelt memories came flooding back with my own stories, but what thrilled me, even more, were the stories from all the others.  I remembered a couple of them fondly, but almost all the others were new to me.  I had no idea my brothers had gone through these experiences.  Once one of the brothers wrote a story, he would submit it and we all got to read it at that time and comment.  This seemed as exciting as or even more so than the completion of the book.  We were riding a wave of emotions every few days and not just all at once.  I now cherish these stories from all six of us.  Remembering as kids some of the brothers would pick on others, as brothers do, but if someone from the neighborhood were to pick on one of the brothers, they would be bombarded by the entire Kearns clan of siblings.  Needless to say, that didn't happen much.  Today, as we are now all adults, we are the best of friends.  When the wives and even the kids are around all six of us, they can't believe the closeness and the silliness of the clan of six.  God has blessed us all and I hope He will bless you too in the reading of these tales.

**Terry**

My thoughts about the book were very much the same as some of my brothers. It allowed me to take time to reflect on some of my experiences from my past and how they have made me the man that I am today.

I must admit that I enjoyed reading the thoughts and feelings that my brothers shared from their perspectives. I hope whoever reads this book will really appreciate the heartfelt stories and maybe consider writing one with their family. May God bless each and every one of you.

**Pat**

I'm not sure whose idea it was to gather life stories from each of the brothers and to compile them into a book, but I guess that doesn't really matter. Living with numerous siblings we learned at a young age that the originator of an idea wasn't as important as acting on an idea, especially when it had to do with having an adventure or just plainly having fun. I feel remarkably blessed to have been raised by two extra-ordinary parents who taught us most significantly by their examples of a lived life. They were far from perfect I could only assume, but how they responded and navigated their imperfections left me, and I would guess my brothers too, with a permanent mark of earned admiration.

As we compiled the stories from the brothers which were received one-by-one over a few months I had the opportunity to read and experience their deep feelings and emotions attached to life events of which some I knew of, but many I did not. As I read about my brother's lives, and their perceptions of events it not only felt familiar and comfortable but also allowed me the opportunity to get to know them more deeply. It was as if I were reading a journal or a diary but with their permission.

I feel that part of the motivation for the creation of the book was to leave a tangible record, a book that could be read and reread by Kearns generations well beyond the short time that many of us have left on this earth. However, it quickly came to my attention that this book is much more than that. It is a reflection of who these six Kearns brothers were/are not only to each other but to the world.

I had always wished my Father had kept a journal and that as I grew in age, I could read about his thoughts and his recollection of many of the experiences of his life. I knew I could learn from his successes and his failures if I had only known about them. Sadly, he abruptly died earlier than most and there was no journal. Well, this collection of stories is in a sense a journal to be shared with our children, nieces, nephews, cousins, and anyone who might find the stories interesting.

**Mike**

I thought this was a great idea from the start! I thought I had heard all the stories that each brother shared but found out that I hadn't heard many of these. It was great to read about all the different adventures each of us had experienced! I feel like our book is a Reflection of our upbringing and the kind of people we turned into. We had an awesome upbringing. Each brother is so caring, compassionate, and are just good people. They honestly would give you the shirt off their back! I know that if we weren't brothers, I would love to have them for friends. You can see our Mom and Dad in each of us. Their influences come out in each of us. You can see why we all get along so well now. We were close growing up (some more than others because of age) and we are closer now. We have a strong "Family Unit" that I am so proud to be a part of! We ARE the "Kearns Boyz 6!" I hope you enjoy reading our book! It brought back great memories from our childhood! I loved reading about my brother's adventures and learning new things that I didn't know about each of my brothers! Thank you, God Bless you!

## Dan

When the idea was brought up about the brothers writing a book together, I was intrigued. It would be something nice and memorable to do as a family. I had no idea that it would come to fruition. It started with a brother or two submitting a story. This led to others writing one, as you didn't want to be outdone or be slacking behind. With life so busy, we moved along at a snail's pace. Here we are today. We finished it.

I've learned so much about my brothers and their journeys through life. Things I never would have known otherwise. I've learned about experiences or memories that are important to them. I've learned about how they feel towards certain things.

I can't help but think how great it would have been to have a book that my Dad and his five brothers wrote. I would have loved to learn more about their thoughts and experiences.

My Mother and her siblings also. It would be something that I could look back on and read when I'm having those periods of missing them so much.

I already know how special my brothers are, but this book has taught me so much more about them. I am so very grateful for how close we all are. The bond that we have is so strong and unbreakable. We may have not been able to take our Ireland trip together this year because of something called Covid and the pandemic, but I'm thankful that we were all still here to write this book together. Thank you to my brothers. I love you.